IMAGES
of America

GAY AND LESBIAN
ATLANTA

ON THE COVER: GRACE THOMAS (LEFT) AND DOROTHY SCHMITZ [VOGEL], ROCK ISLAND, ILLINOIS, 1931. Many lesbians and gay men born in the first half of the 20th century dutifully conformed to traditional roles. They often married, raised families, and only later acknowledged desires and identities that had remained unspoken. For others, self-awareness at an early age allowed them to follow a different course. Throughout her life, Dorothy Vogel's most significant, intimate relationships would be with women. (Courtesy Kenan Research Center at the Atlanta History Center.)

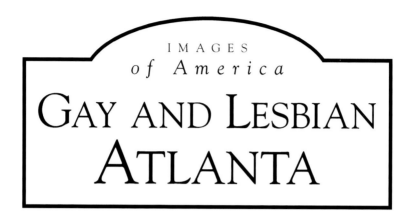

IMAGES
of America

GAY AND LESBIAN ATLANTA

Wesley Chenault and Stacy Braukman
Atlanta History Center

ARCADIA
PUBLISHING

Published by Arcadia Publishing
Charleston, South Carolina

Printed in the United States of America

Library of Congress Catalog Card Number: 2007940692

For all general information contact Arcadia Publishing at:
Telephone 843-853-2070
Fax 843-853-0044
E-mail sales@arcadiapublishing.com
For customer service and orders:
Toll-Free 1-888-313-2665

Visit us on the Internet at www.arcadiapublishing.com

To our friends and families

CONTENTS

ACKNOWLEDGMENTS

This project would not have been possible without the counsel, generosity, and forethought of many people. Terry Bird, María Helena Dolan, Cal Gough, David Hayward, John Howard, Gil Robison, Liz Throop, and Joy Wasson, along with the other members of the Atlanta Lesbian and Gay History Thing, are responsible for the collection that makes up the foundation for much of this book.

Many oral history participants, including Jeff Askew, Allen Jones, Richard Kavanaugh, Diamond Lil, Charlene McLemore, William Penn, Freddie Styles, Jack Strouss, and Barbara Vogel, gave diaries, photograph albums, and other memorabilia in addition to their personal stories. Without volunteer support from Hugo Berston, Jim Ford, Mary Anne Melear, and Joey Orr, among others, the oral history and archival collections would not be what they are today.

Donations by Delia Champion and Wendy Weiner, Kristal Manning and Melinda McBride, John Meeks and John Townsend, Suellen Parker and Allison Shockley, Kristin Reichman (Southern Comfort Conference), Jeri and John Sassany, Sherry Siclair, Alli Royce Soble, and Cathy Woolard helped fill in gaps for recent decades.

Friends, scholars, and others unstintingly shared their knowledge and connections, among them Doug Carl, Duane Coleman, Lewis Covington, Richard Funderburke, Don Hunnewell, Mark Jordan, Cliff Lietch, Renee Palmer and Patsy McGirl, Jodie Talley, and Dixon Taylor. Several archivists lent institutional support: William Holden, Karen Jefferson, Elizabeth Knowlton, Peter Roberts, and Kerrie Williams. Thanks to Maggie Tiller Bullwinkle, our editor at Arcadia Publishing, for shepherding this project with patience and thoughtful suggestions.

The staff of the Kenan Research Center cheerfully adapted to many mood swings. Those who suffered the most with the greatest patience were Staci L. Catron, Paul Crater, Betsy Rix, and Michael Rose.

Three special angels—Kathy Freise, Rebecca Hernandez, and Michele Potter—sent much-needed *besos y abrazos* from the Southwest.

Finally, we thank our partners, John Ryan and Beth Mauldin, for sharing their love and for tolerating our shenanigans.

INTRODUCTION

This book originated with the Atlanta History Center exhibition *The Unspoken Past: Atlanta Lesbian and Gay History, 1940–1970*, which brought to life one small portion of the city's gay history through photographs and printed materials. The research and oral histories conducted for the exhibit suggested that much of the larger story remained to be told. Based on the exhibit's popularity, and in response to the many comments asking to see more of the collection, the staff sought a project that would expand on the themes of *The Unspoken Past* exhibition, cover a broader historical range, and, with any luck, reach a wider audience.

The James G. Kenan Research Center at the Atlanta History Center began collecting material in the early 1990s with the help of the Atlanta Lesbian and Gay History Thing. The center is currently engaged in ongoing, intensive outreach to bolster this significant repository of archival resources, including photographs, personal papers, and organizational records. Drawing on these visual materials and oral history interviews, *Gay and Lesbian Atlanta* explores the lived experiences of generations of gay and lesbian Atlantans during the 20th century.

The history of a place, a group of people, or political and social change can never be neat and tidy. It can never proceed in a straight line or follow an unswerving trajectory. Yet in the study of gay and lesbian history in this country, it is tempting to interpret a general movement away from ignorance and repression at the beginning of the 20th century toward enlightened acceptance on the part of the people, the laws, and the institutions at the end of it. One could argue convincingly that such a movement has indeed taken place. A list of the ways that life has improved for lesbians and gays would be exhaustive. But the movement has occurred in fits and starts, for some groups more quickly than others, and at times with mixed results and unintended consequences.

On a national level, historians have documented periods of acute anxiety about homosexuality during the 20th century. Whether during the "sexual psychopath" scares of the 1920s and 1930s, the government and military purges during World War II and the Cold War, or the rising tide of cultural conservatism that began in the 1960s and showed few signs of cresting even as the century drew to a close, there have been discernible ebbs and flows in the polity's preoccupation with homosexuality as a social ill. By the same token, historians have also noted those moments when definitions, beliefs, and laws became less discriminatory and when individuals maneuvered through systems of oppression to create communities and live fulfilling lives. Depending on individuals' circumstances and context, they might not have experienced a moment's fear during the 1950s or they may have remained closeted during the 1990s—a time of unprecedented cultural popularity, if not downright trendiness, of being gay.

The stories that comprise the history of gay and lesbian Atlanta touch on all of these issues and many more (though in some ways fewer). By virtue of its location in the Deep South, shaped as it was by the values of a Protestant, slaveholding society and in spite of its early industrial leanings, the city started out as a small railroad town in the middle of the 19th century. Its total population remained modest by national standards as the next century dawned. It did attract industry, trade, and transportation but not many foreign immigrants. As it expanded, Atlanta in many ways stayed rooted in its provincial origins. That is to say, throughout much of the 20th century, Atlanta was no New York, San Francisco, or Chicago.

It was, however, a regional center, and after World War II, Atlanta became one of a handful of prominent Sun Belt metropolitan areas in which conservative political values coexisted with ever-larger numbers of educated, professional people who were more likely to be socially liberal. It is no coincidence that gay networks and culture emerged in Atlanta as the city grew rapidly during the postwar years and as new residents and tourists streamed in from other parts of the country.

There is no single profile that fits gay and lesbian Atlantans. They came from around the South and around the country, arriving from small towns, large cities, and suburbs. Their experiences and opportunities were and continue to be influenced by race, gender, and economics. Many survived hardships by forging intimate personal relationships and close-knit social networks, and lived through crucial shifts in attitudes, laws, and political climates. Their narratives—of adversity and triumph, of isolation and community, and of struggle and pride—were all shaped in part by the experience of living in Atlanta. Indeed, the histories of these men and women are inseparable from the history of the city itself.

The images presented here attempt to capture the breadth and complexity of gay life in Atlanta during the last century. While the majority of the materials come from the collections housed at the James G. Kenan Research Center, in some instances material from other institutions appears and is acknowledged. Since this is a pictorial history, editorial and layout constraints prohibit a comprehensive presentation or discussion. Instead, this book offers a selection of photographs that represent both well-known and rarely seen moments from the city's past. Unless noted, all images depict Atlanta; photographers are credited when known. Whenever possible, the authors have included the actual voices of gay and lesbian Atlantans to allow them to tell their own compelling stories.

One

UNCONVENTIONAL LIVES
AND
AMBIGUOUS IDENTITIES
1900–1940

From the turn of the 20th century through the 1930s, Atlanta showed few, if any, signs of a distinct gay culture. Atlanta had become an important regional center of transportation, commerce, and industry. During this period, its population grew threefold, approaching 300,000 by the height of the Depression. Physically, Atlanta expanded along with the populace as streetcars and later automobiles carried city dwellers to outlying neighborhoods such as Brookhaven, East Lake, and Grant Park.

People who moved to the city from other parts of the South enjoyed not only employment, but also a host of entertainment options not likely offered in the small towns and rural communities from which they had come. Vaudeville and burlesque shows, movie houses, and bars and saloons all offered cheap amusements for the working and middle classes.

This chapter explores fragmentary photographic and journalistic evidence of same-sex relationships, cross-dressing, and other unconventional modes of gender and sexual identification in Atlanta. Lingering Victorian notions of romantic friendship for both men and women complicate modern interpretations of same-sex intimacy. In the past, particularly during the early 20th century when there was scarcely a vocabulary for making sense of same-sex desire, gay men and lesbians often self-censored or destroyed their letters, photographs, and other primary sources of historical value.

DOWNTOWN ATLANTA, 1895. At the end of the 19th century, Atlanta was still a relatively small city, but it was growing rapidly as economic opportunities expanded and newcomers poured in from across the South in search of work. By 1900, Atlanta's population stood at nearly 90,000. It would rise to 150,000 within a decade. This growth exceeded the national average, and though Atlanta was the largest city in Georgia, it was still outsized by Nashville and New Orleans. African Americans made up about 40 percent of the population, but legalized racial segregation kept blacks and whites separate in public transportation and accommodations, neighborhoods, jobs, and schools. Despite white civic and business leaders' efforts to sell Atlanta as a model city of the New South—a modern, progressive, industrializing beacon—at the end of the 19th century, the city remained firmly grounded in Old South racial customs.

FIVE POINTS, 1914. Five Points served as the commercial and cultural center of early Atlanta with the meeting of the city's major thoroughfares: Whitehall, Decatur, Edgewood, Marietta, and Peachtree Streets. In the late 19th and early 20th centuries, Decatur Street was the heart of Atlanta's African American working-class entertainment district, brimming with saloons, bars, and dance halls. When the Georgia legislature banned alcohol consumption in 1908, however, many of these establishments were shut down. This was part of a larger debate during this period among city leaders and citizens about the nature of commercial culture and Atlanta's reputation. Members of such organizations as the Film Censorship Board and the Evangelical Ministers' Association argued that new commercialized amusements like vaudeville, burlesque, and movies were dangerously immoral and threatened the city's Christian values.

THE CAPITOL AND GEORGIA THEATERS, 1929. By the end of the 1930s, this part of Peachtree Street was commonly known as the theater district. Other well-known theaters nearby included the Paramount (formerly the Howard) and Loew's Grand. With the increasing availability and popularity of automobiles came busier streets and new pressures for improving the city's roads and other infrastructure. Increased mobility would later bring gays and lesbians together at various gathering places and private homes for purposes of socializing as well as sex. Atlanta resident Virginia Boyd described how a car turned out to be the setting for a pivotal moment in her life during the early 1940s as a recent high school graduate. As Boyd and her companion sat and talked in the privacy of an automobile, her friend said, "'Bless your heart, you sounded so forlorn, I almost kissed you.' And I said—I'll never know why I did this—I said, 'Why didn't you?' And so she did."

PEACHTREE ARCADE (AT LEFT), C. 1939. The Great Depression hit Georgia and the rest of the South hard. In 1938, Pres. Franklin Roosevelt famously called the region the "number one economic problem" in the country. While Georgia and the South benefited from a number of New Deal programs, people continued flocking to Atlanta from rural areas affected by falling farm prices, foreclosures, and unemployment. In many ways, the city retained a small-town sensibility. But it also received millions of dollars in federal funds, including the job-providing Works Progress Administration (WPA) and the nation's first low-income public housing projects: Techwood Homes for whites and University Homes for African Americans. In the face of national and regional economic catastrophe, Atlanta began to pull out of the Depression by the end of the 1930s as private businesses and industry grew and banks reopened.

EVENTFUL CAREER OF A WOMAN WHO BECAME "FEMALE HUSBAND"

Wore Men's Clothing, Smoked Chewed and Shaved—Became a "Bridegroom" Before Her Secret Was Discovered.

KANSAS CITY, Mo.—Of all the strange stories which come before the police departments of big cities, none is recalled in which officers were forced to tell a bride of three days that her "husband" is a woman, as was the case when "John A. Whitman," arrested here as a vagrant, turned out to be Pauline Webster, 21, Gaffney City, S. C.

The bride, Etta Jelley, refused at first to believe the statement, and later burst into tears of humiliation and of sorrow.

Etta loved "John," and after "his" arrest held "his" hand, brought "him" delicacies and otherwise conducted herself as any bride of three days might have done under the circumstances.

The "female husband" took things calmly. Smoking a cigarette and chewing a cud of tobacco, two habits she had forced herself to acquire, she calmly sat on the edge of a bunk in a cell.

Miss Jelley, aged 25, is a waitress.

"This person—John, Joseph, Pauline or whatever you want to call him—I mean her—told me we would put our money together and start a restaurant. He—I mean she—said he had some money in the bank, and that she was born in Paris. I had saved up $185, which Cornett was keeping for me. Cornett would not give me the money even after we saw the justice of the peace. I am glad of it now. Cornett saved me."

The climax of the wedding was caused by Cornett. After Miss Jelley tried to get her $185, Cornett investigated and found that "Whitman" had pleaded illness after the ceremony and had made no prep-

PAULINE WEBSTER, "FEMALE HUSBAND."

ATLANTA JOURNAL, FEBRUARY 10, 1906. Stories like this one from Kansas City, Missouri, appeared occasionally in the Atlanta press, revealing an interest in ambiguous gender practices. In a city dominated by evangelical Protestant ideals of sexual propriety and traditional gender roles, these tales offered a titillating glimpse into the forbidden, alien realm of cross-dressing and same-sex relationships.

ATLANTA CONSTITUTION, JULY 24, 1913. The *Constitution* examined the issue of gender conventions in this article about Anthony Auriemma, a professional female impersonator who contested Atlanta's city ordinance banning public cross-dressing. Though the story was reported in a humorous tone, it revealed the popularity of gender nonconformity within the socially acceptable context of the era's cheap amusements.

Is It Lady-Like to Look Like A Lady on Atlanta's Streets

Is it proper, also is it legal, for a real ladylike man to further simulate femininity and appear on the streets dressed in woman's garb, provided this man be a professional female impersonator?

This is a question which is troubling Miss—beg your pardon—Mr. Auriema, who is nightly appearing at one of Atlanta's moving picture show houses. Also it is troubling Chief Beavers.

If it is proper and legal for a woman to cut her hair and don male costume as did Belva Lockwood and Dr. Mary Walker, who, for many years, were conspicuous figures in New York, Washington and other populous centers, why shouldn't I take the place of some of the women who are fast abandoning the frills and furbelows so long cherished by womankind?

This is the way that Mr. Auriema argued.

"Really," he said to himself, "if women keep on deserting the ranks

IT LOOKS LIKE A WOMAN—IT WALKS LIKE A WOMAN—BY GUM! I DELIEVE IT IS A WOMAN!

If Auriema has her (that is his) wa

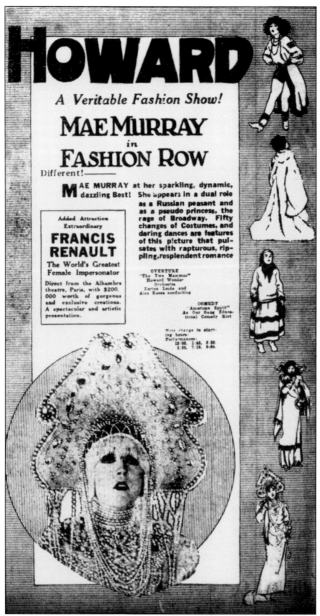

ATLANTA CONSTITUTION, JANUARY 13, 1924. By the 1920s, Atlanta newspapers were publishing advertisements for a motion picture at the Howard Theatre (later the Paramount) that featured Francis Renault, the "world's greatest female impersonator." Renault, whose real name was Anthony Auriemma, was an immensely popular vaudeville performer. He had challenged Atlanta police chief James Beavers for the right to walk down the street in high heels 11 years earlier. This change in attitude in a relatively short period is even more remarkable considering the legacy of the Atlanta race riot in 1906, an outburst of anti-black violence that came on the heels of the city's white newspapers publishing sensational accounts of alleged Negro rapes and assaults on white women.

WOMEN DANCING AND EMBRACING, c. 1915. Making historical sense of same-sex relationships during earlier centuries presents many challenges. Modern definitions of sexuality are often dramatically different from those of other eras. During the late 19th and early 20th centuries, lingering Victorian notions of romantic friendships between people of the same sex shaped the way that the two white women pictured at left, as well as the subjects in the photographs that follow, would have been viewed at the time. Intense emotional relationships, for both men and women, were not imbued with sexual connotations, but in later decades, they would come under closer scrutiny and criticism. This standard also applied to African American women (below), who could enjoy close relationships with members of the same sex under the custom of romantic friendships.

MAN IN THE MOON AND MEN EMBRACING, C. 1920. The scenery at right, called the Man in the Moon, was typically used as a backdrop by studios, traveling photographers, and carnivals. In most cases, the stage set was employed to signify sweethearts. The presentation of the two African American men together below and, more generally, any displays of affection between men would likely not have raised eyebrows in the early 20th century, even in Atlanta and the South. These photographs further complicate reading historical images through modern eyes, especially when the subjects and the provenance of the images remain unknown to the viewer. When biographical information is available, however, as is the case with the set of images that follows, the implication is less speculative than suggestive of same-sex relationships.

FRIENDS OF DOROTHY SCHMITZ, C. 1928. Florence "Squid" Reeves, pictured above in Beaufort, South Carolina, was a friend to Schmitz, who moved to Atlanta in the 1930s and whose most significant relationships were with women. Though Reeves's sexuality is unknown, her boyish hairstyle and clothing could be markers of the modern woman of the 1920s, but they may be expressions of her sexual identity as well. The concept of the "modern woman" opened up a cultural space in which women could play with gender roles and conventions, and blur the lines between acceptable femininity and illicit mannishness. The unidentified women pictured left at Watchaug Pond, Rhode Island, were also part of Schmitz's circle of friends.

JACK STROUSS, 1937 (RIGHT) AND 1941 (BELOW, RIGHT). Strouss first recognized his difference from other teenagers while attending Atlanta's Technological High School. He soon became aware of his same-sex yearnings, and to his surprised delight, he met "a couple or three fellows that seemed to be friendly and sort of gravitated toward me and vice versa, and that was my slow but easy introduction to what I was, my orientation. These were nice fellows and local people, so we just hung around together and I began to be informed about what was going on." His first exposure to gay gatherings also occurred during high school when his friend Charles Braswell (below, left) took him to the Lounge, a popular nightspot in downtown Atlanta where small groups of gay men commonly socialized.

NORRIS BUMSTEAD HERNDON, 1926. The son of African Americans Alonzo and Adrienne Herndon, Norris was born in 1897. Educated at Atlanta University and the Harvard Business School, he worked at his father's business, the Atlanta Life Insurance Company. When Norris's father died in 1927, he assumed the presidency and oversaw the company's greatest period of growth. Norris's sexuality was considered an open secret among his friends and colleagues.

THE HERNDON HOME, 1988. Building on his father's legacy, Norris Herndon established the Alonzo F. and Norris B. Herndon Foundation in 1950, contributing millions of dollars to both local and national African American educational, charitable, and religious organizations. The foundation also supports the Herndon mansion, designated a National Historic Landmark in 2000. (Photograph by William F. Hull.)

ATLANTA LIFE INSURANCE COMPANY, C. 1955. A symbol of African American entrepreneurship and Atlanta's African American elite, Atlanta Life was founded in 1905 and headquartered on Auburn Avenue, the historic center of African American business and culture beginning in the early 20th century. In 1955, *Ebony* magazine profiled Norris Herndon as one of the most eligible African American bachelors in the country. The article emphasized Herndon's secrecy and elusiveness, calling him "the millionaire nobody knows," a man "available to a select group of intimates and executives, who guard his whereabouts with the passion of secret service men protecting the president." His reticence is not surprising given the repressive climate of the McCarthy era and his position as the sole heir to an African American fortune in a racially divided city. In *Atlanta Life Insurance Company* (1990), Alexa Benson Henderson argues that "a distinctive humanitarian and philanthropic influence emanated from Norris," and he "chose to make his participation quiet and unobtrusive."

DOROTHY SCHMITZ (TOP) AND GRACE THOMAS, 1932. Dot, as friends knew her, is pictured here with Grace, a close friend and confidant, performing an elaborate dive at the Venetian Club. Founded in 1931, the club became a popular recreational spot for white Atlantans.

ORRIN AND DOROTHY VOGEL, 1934. Dorothy Schmitz, sitting on Stone Mountain, married Orrin Vogel (standing), an engineer for Georgia Power, in 1934. They had two daughters, Barbara and Patricia. The couple divorced in 1939, six months after Barbara was born. Throughout the rest of her life, Dorothy's romantic relationships were with women.

DOROTHY SCHMITZ, 1925 AND 1927.
Dorothy Schmitz (pictured at right wearing a hat) and a friend visit Webster Lake, New Hampshire. The image captures Dorothy's affinity for mannish dress and sensibilities, as well as her outward refusal to bow to social norms. As her daughter Barbara recalled later, "The very remarkable thing about my mother—and that I really respected her for, though at the time I thought it was really weird—was that she wore flannel shirts and blue jeans and loafers, and she drove trucks." Shown below with friends at Camp Watchaug, Rhode Island, Dorothy (far right) was a sports and outdoors enthusiast, enjoying swimming, tennis, and horseback riding.

17 BALTIMORE BLOCK, 1939 AND C. 1935. The photograph above was taken during the three-day festivities surrounding the Atlanta premiere of *Gone With the Wind*. In the 1920s and 1930s, Baltimore Block was home to a vibrant assortment of artists, photographers, landscape architects, and antiques dealers. It also provided a comfortable space for sexual nonconformists, among them Harvey M. Smith Jr., an interior decorator whose studio was located at 17 Baltimore Place between West Peachtree and Spring Streets. The image at left depicts the interior of the home where Smith lived.

HARVEY SMITH, C. 1915 AND c. 1930. Smith was born in Atlanta in 1906 and attended Emory and Oglethorpe Universities. At right, a young Smith visits his family's farm in Danway, Alabama. Below, wearing a white shirt, he performs onstage at the Studio Club in Atlanta. Following his service in the U.S. Marine Corps, Smith moved to New York City in 1958, where he purchased Patterson Fabrics, a design firm specializing in curtains and wallpaper. Between 1936 and 1938, he published *The Southern Architectural Review* and began an extensive collection of rare architecture and decorative arts books. His collection, which includes photographs and personal papers, was later donated to the Atlanta History Center.

CHARLES BRASWELL, C. 1940; GRACE THOMAS AND DOROTHY SCHMITZ [VOGEL], 1931.
Atlanta is the transportation hub of the region. During the early 20th century, increasing numbers of automobiles joined railroads and streetcars in the transportation of goods and people. The city's expansion of roads connected downtown with the suburbs and rural areas, and allowed individuals to cross cultural, geographic, and social lines. The automobile provided opportunities for leisure activities beyond the home and reshaped dating habits. For many, the automobile provided an escape from the surveillance of parents, the police, or spouses.

DECATUR STREET, C. 1938. Though many African American saloons and bars on Decatur had been shut down after the race riot of 1906, it remained an important, if subdued, entertainment hub in the 1920s and 1930s. Pictured at center right is 81 Theater, one of Atlanta's best-known nightclubs. Owned by white businessman Charles Bailey, the club featured a wide range of African American music and dance from jazz and blues, to vaudeville, and later to Broadway numbers. Gertrude "Ma" Rainey, Bessie Smith, and Ethel Waters were among its legendary performers. Rainey hailed from Columbus, Georgia, and after a successful vaudeville career, she became a groundbreaking blues writer and singer. She was one of the first women blues performers to record her own compositions. Though married, Rainey was openly bisexual; her song "Prove It on Me" (1928) includes references to cross-dressing and sexual attraction to women.

FORSYTH STREET, 1926. Throughout the 1940s, the Vocalis family owned and operated the Lounge and an adjacent liquor store. A neon-lit sign that read "Lounge" made the establishment visible on Forsyth Street. According to Jack Strouss, the Lounge was one of the first establishments to get a beer and wine license after Prohibition ended in the city. Charles Vocalis, Strouss remembered, "was very nice, ran a very tight ship, nice place, but nice people, had two sons who helped him in the afternoon after school." Inside, Charles and his sons tended a long bar that occupied the left side of the room. Down a narrow passage past the bar, Helen Vocalis sat in a stand selling cigarettes and sundries. Out of view from the entry and hallway were booths where Strouss and his friends gathered.

Two

QUIET ACCOMMODATION
1940–1970

World War II was a watershed in nearly every realm of American life. Thousands of men and women from Atlanta joined the service, and those who stayed behind found employment in defense work, participated in civil defense, and sacrificed many of the creature comforts of a consumer culture on behalf of the war effort.

After 1945, with the return of GIs to colleges, offices, and suburbs, transportation in Atlanta experienced rapid growth. In turn, individuals experienced greater movement and freedom to cross cultural, geographical, and social lines. Candler Field, the forerunner to Hartsfield-Jackson International Airport, expanded its facilities and services. Expressways began to crisscross the city, eventually linking with major interstate highways. Increasing numbers of cars appeared, enabling movement between downtown and the suburbs, rural and urban locations, "colored" and "white" areas, and cultural and domestic spheres.

Between 1940 and 1970 in Atlanta, sexual identity was rarely publicly articulated by gays and lesbians themselves (though it was condemned periodically by the police and the church) and rarely politicized. Unlike other cities in the Northeast and on the West Coast, there were no known homophile organizations in Atlanta. For some men and women, the single-sex environment of the armed services made them aware that they were not alone in their same-sex desire and behavior.

Instead, from the 1940s through the 1960s, quiet social networks of men and women existed throughout the city. These private bonds, of which few spoke publicly, were not always connected; they often split along lines of gender, age, race, and class. They were, however, a source of hope, strength, and love. At a time when coming out brought the possibility of social and familial ostracism, religious condemnation, or even criminal prosecution, there existed a climate of quiet accommodation. This social environment allowed lesbians and gays to identify and connect with one another, albeit discreetly.

BELL BOMBER, C. 1944. The Bell Aircraft Corporation opened this aircraft manufacturing facility in Marietta in 1943, and for the next two years, workers built more than 600 B-29 bombers for the country's use in World War II. Located 20 miles north of Atlanta, the company provided thousands of jobs to those who had lived through the privations of the Depression. A vast majority of employees were Southerners, mostly from Georgia. More than a third of the workforce was

made up of women, and six percent were African Americans. Bell Bomber epitomized the massive wartime funneling of U.S. Defense Department funds and resources into the South, for the first time drawing middle-class white women into the labor force and creating new social opportunities and greater financial freedom for workers.

VIRGINIA BOYD, 1942. Pictured here in *The Skyscraper*, the Commercial High School yearbook, Boyd joined the navy in 1944 when she was 20 years old. She remembered going to off-limits clubs during basic training and seeing female officers dancing together: "And so you'd dance with them, too. . . . You'd kind of have a little secret. But you don't tell on them, and they don't tell on you."

JACK STROUSS, BAD NAUHEIM, GERMANY, 1945. During his military service, Strouss frequently played piano for troops in European clubs operated by the Red Cross. Here he is seen at a Noncommissioned Officers Club in the small resort town of Bad Nauheim, just north of Frankfurt. Strouss recalled fondly his days as an entertainer when "nice fellows would hang around the piano, and you'd get to know more people that way."

UNIDENTIFIED WOMEN AND MEN, C. 1945. Thousands of gay men and lesbians served in America's armed forces during World War II. In this environment, they became familiar with the military's anti-homosexual policies and psychiatric models of abnormal sexuality. As a result, lesbians and gay men were mindful of what they said and how they behaved, though it did not stop them from congregating. For some, the single-sex environment provided opportunities to act on and express sexual desire, fall in love, make friends, and exchange thoughts and information about who they were.

TIM JOHNSON, C. 1945, AND JACK STROUSS, 1945. Tim (at left in Guam) and Jack (below in France) dated during high school, but the war kept them apart until 1945 when they reunited at Tim's home on Highland Avenue. Jack Strouss remembered that he "jumped out of that Ford and ran up that porch. Tim came running out, and we hugged closely, right there on the porch. His mama was standing there weeping." By 1946, however, the two had begun to grow apart, and soon Strouss was in a relationship with Donald Ross, a close friend from the service. "We did everything, and we shared so much," recalled Strouss.

TIM JOHNSON AND JACK STROUSS, 1942. This souvenir photograph, taken at the Shangri-La Restaurant on Luckie Street in downtown Atlanta, shows Tim (far right) and Jack (third from right) with some of their heterosexual friends during a typical night out on the town. Upon his return from Europe, Strouss rejoined his friends and resumed a favorite social activity, dancing. Atlanta had not changed significantly during Strouss's absence, and he was eager to return to the busy social life he had enjoyed before the war. He explained, "We called all those girls, and we were dancing within a week, finding all the places we used to go. We just had our girlfriends so that we could dance, and we [males] did not dance together much—occasionally, if we were in a home or something. But we would go to the other places with all of our friends."

DOROTHY VOGEL AND ELIZABETH BOWLES, 1942. When Dorothy Vogel (left) divorced her husband in 1939, her infant daughter Barbara lived with her. For the rest of her life, Dorothy had intimate relationships with other women. Her most significant partner was Elizabeth Bowles, seen here holding Barbara.

YWCA STAFF CONFERENCE, C. 1942. Both Elizabeth Bowles and Dorothy Vogel joined the YWCA staff in 1942, and the two soon became romantically involved. Here Elizabeth sits in the first row, second from right, while Dorothy sits third from the left in the third row. Barbara admired her mother's individuality and nonconformity, for being "who she was." As she put it, "I learned a lot from that."

ALLEN O. JONES AND PHILIP HEISLER, c. 1945. Born in 1937, Allen O. Jones (left) graduated from Georgia Tech in 1960 and served in the U.S. Air Force Reserve. He later became chairman of the Georgia Federation of Young Republican Clubs and worked as an investment banker and political organizer. In 1992, Jones founded the Atlanta Executive Network, a gay and lesbian business and professional organization.

FREDDIE STYLES WITH HIS GRANDMOTHER AND SISTER, 1953. Freddie Styles was born in Madison, Georgia, in 1944. In 1952, when his grandmother Effie Bynum became ill, his family moved to the Summerhill neighborhood of Atlanta. Styles attended Price Luther Judson High School and Morris Brown College.

GUY DOBBS AND JEFF ASKEW, 1946 (ABOVE); DONALD ROSS AND JACK STROUSS, 1948 (BELOW). In the post–World War II period, many lesbians and gay men conformed to traditional roles, marrying and raising families. Others chose a different path. Guy Dobbs (above, left) and Jeff Askew met at Fort McPherson and became good friends. Following the war, each married and raised families. Guy and Emily Dobbs later divorced, and both came out privately. After his wife's passing in the early 1990s, Askew came out publicly and began a long-term relationship with another man. Some, like Jack Strouss (below, right), never conformed and married, instead choosing same-sex relationships exclusively.

BILLY JONES, C. 1947. Born in Griffin, Georgia, Billy Jones moved to Atlanta with his family in the late 1920s. His earliest memories involved the city's theaters. Jones recalled that going to the Fox Theatre was "the first thing we did when we got to Atlanta." In 1936, he and his brother walked several miles to see a Myrna Loy film at the Fox. "We walked and we walked and we walked, and it was the longest walk ever in my life," he remembered. "We sat through it twice, but when we came out it was dark, so we caught the streetcar back home. I never made that walk again." Following his military service during World War II, Jones worked for 30 years at the Franklin Simon department store, where he would become known for his traffic-stopping window designs. After he and his wife divorced in the late 1950s, Jones came out to his closest friends. In the mid-1960s, using the stage names Phyllis Killer and Shirley Temple Jones, he became a popular female impersonator.

SACRED HEART CATHOLIC CHURCH, C. 1955. In the mid-1940s, George Hyde was dismissed from seminary school for homosexuality and moved to Atlanta, where he attended Sacred Heart Catholic Church. In 1946, when a gay church member was publicly shunned, Hyde and 20 men and women began holding informal services at the Winecoff Hotel. It provided a supportive environment for those who believed in Hyde's message of tolerance.

LUCY WOOD CAFETERIA, c. 1950. When some church members were fired after being arrested for "disorderly conduct" at a private party, George Hyde rallied his network of supporters to help. Among them was Lucy Wood, the owner and proprietor of a popular downtown cafeteria. (Courtesy Special Collections Department and Archives, Georgia State University Library.)

CARNEGIE LIBRARY, 1954. Located at the corner of Forsyth Street and Carnegie Way in downtown Atlanta, the Carnegie Library opened in 1902. In September 1953, during an eight-day stakeout of the men's restroom, the Atlanta Police Department arrested 20 men on felony charges of sodomy. Their names and addresses appeared in the city's newspapers on more than one occasion, and all but one lost their jobs as a result. The men were also fined and received suspended sentences. The Atlanta Public Library Perversion Case, as the *Atlanta Constitution* called it, was one of numerous crackdowns on public spaces used by homosexuals, including bars, restrooms, bus stations, and parks, during the 1950s. These efforts resulted from public anxiety over sex and sexuality after World War II and coincided with the military's continuing exclusionary policy and the federal government's purges of gay men and lesbians from its ranks.

LILLIAN SMITH, 1944. Lillian Smith was 18 years old when her family moved to Clayton, Georgia, to operate the Laurel Falls Camp for Girls. There Smith met Paula Snelling, who became her lifelong companion. In 1936, the two began publishing a quarterly magazine, which they used as a platform against segregation. Her first novel, *Strange Fruit* (1944), depicts an interracial relationship that is ultimately punished by a brutal lynching. With three million copies sold, the novel became the No. 1 fiction bestseller of 1944. Lillian Smith died in Atlanta in September 1966. In 1968, the Southern Regional Council began presenting the Lillian Smith Book Award to works that further the understanding of human rights and social issues. Since 2004, the award has been presented in partnership with the University of Georgia Libraries. (Courtesy Library of Congress.)

DANIEL WHITEHEAD HICKY, C. 1949.
Born in 1900, Hicky moved to Atlanta
when he was 19. A frequent contributor
to *The Saturday Evening Post*, he also
served as president of the Atlanta Writers'
Club. In the 1930s and 1940s, Hicky
wrote a gossip column, "Crackers and
Crumbs," which followed the goings-
on at the Piedmont Driving Circle, the
Capital City Club, the East Lake Country
Club, and other exclusive social clubs.

**DONALD WINDHAM AND SANDY
CAMPBELL, NEW YORK, 1955.** Born
in Atlanta in 1920, Donald Windham
(left) moved to New York with Fred
Melton in 1939. There he became
friends with Tennessee Williams,
Truman Capote, and other authors.
Windham met Sandy Campbell in
1943, and the couple's relationship
lasted until Campbell's death in 1988.
Windham's short stories appeared
in numerous magazines, and he is
the author or editor of 12 books.
(Courtesy Library of Congress.)

DOWNTOWN ATLANTA, 1950. This view of Peachtree Street, looking south, captures some of the vibrancy of nightlife in postwar Atlanta, particularly downtown. Among the theaters, hotels, nightclubs, and restaurants, many lesbians and gays had favorite spots where they would gather and socialize. In an era before the existence of openly gay bars, these venues provided valuable sources of community, though for whites only. The Tick Tock Grill, commonly referred to as Tick Tock, was a diner that featured a "short order cook . . . bar, and booths, and jukebox," just north of downtown at 1935 Peachtree Road. As Virginia Boyd recalled, "We were there more than we were at home!" Amid the hum of the present-day Margaret Mitchell Square at Peachtree and Forsyth Streets, the Five O'Clock Supper Club opened on the second floor of 160 Peachtree, across from the Paramount and Loew's Grand Theaters.

CLUB PEACHTREE, MID-1950s. Popularized in the 1940s, supper clubs were semiformal entertainment establishments offering dining, dancing, and nightclub performances. Opened between 1948 and 1949, the Five O'Clock Supper Club became Club Peachtree in 1951. As George Hyde described, "There was a large contingency of gays working at Davison Paxon, at Rich's department store, at some of the downtown insurance offices—office boys. . . . They would congregate and meet at the Five O' Clock Supper Club," which according to Hyde "was gay for the cocktail hour. After six o'clock, it became non-gay. So they'd meet in there for drinks, then they'd go home, change clothes, take a shower, come back to town and go" to favorite hotel bars.

WONDER CLUB SOUVENIR COVER, 1946. In 1955, Guy Dobbs managed the Queen of Clubs in Atlanta, hosting female impersonators like Bobbie La Marr, who traveled with the Jewel Box Revue and appeared at the Wonder Club in New Orleans.

QUEEN OF CLUBS ADVERTISEMENT, 1955. The Queen of Clubs touted its specialty in featuring female impersonators as "a bit of 'Gay Southland' transposed to Atlanta's Most Unique Club." Within the context of the supper club, gay club managers and female impersonators were part of Atlanta's nightlife, though in modest numbers, in the 1950s.

GUY DOBBS, FIVE O'CLOCK SUPPER CLUB, C. 1951. Advertisements for downtown restaurants and supper clubs, including the Five O'Clock Supper Club, appeared in *Gay Atlanta*, the city's first nightlife circular, which began publication in 1937. At that time, the popular use of the word *gay* meant "happy" or "lively," and this guide featured entertainment and attractions, points of interest, jokes, a downtown map, and local information. Convention and travel centers, hotels, restaurants, and the Atlanta Chamber of Commerce distributed it. In addition to managing supper clubs during the 1950s, Guy Dobbs also performed in drag, first as Little Gwendolyn at the Five O'Clock Supper Club and Club Peachtree. He later changed his drag name to Terry Lynn. During the 1950s and for most of the 1960s, drag shows took place in straight venues, and gays and lesbians created their own spaces there.

HOUSE PARTIES, 1955 (ABOVE) AND 1958 (BELOW). Cocktail parties and dinners were popular forms of socializing among middle- and upper-class lesbians and gays in Atlanta during the 1950s and into the 1960s. They offered private spaces where people could visit with friends, meet new people, and not be subjected to disapproving scrutiny, particularly in the era before gay bars. The gatherings took place regularly, as Bill Weaver remembers. "We had dinner parties at least once a week, and sometimes twice, with friends, and those friends introduced us to other friends, and it was all sort of by word of mouth." He adds, "It was in these home meetings that you met other gay people."

MRS. P'S ADVERTISEMENT, 1956. Hubert and Vera Phillips managed the Piedmont Tavern on Piedmont Avenue. During the 1950s, the site became a gathering place for lesbians who played softball in Piedmont Park. "They're the ones that first opened up the Piedmont Tavern to our gay crowd," and then "the men started going too," Jack Strouss recalled. In 1956, the Phillips couple opened Mrs. P's, a bar in the Ponce de Leon Hotel.

CAMELLIA GARDEN ADVERTISEMENT, 1959. The Wisteria Garden Cocktail Lounge was located in the back of the Camellia Garden Restaurant, located at 1851 Peachtree Road. In the 1950s, Jack Strouss started noticing more gay customers. "And then this crowd of people began to come in after ten o'clock when the restaurant closed, congregating in the back of the dining room where the bar was," he remembered. "It was quite a gathering place."

BILLY DOBBS AND FRIENDS, NEW ORLEANS, LOUISIANA, 1957. Pictured from left to right are Emily Dobbs, Billy Dobbs, Joey ?, and Mary Ellen Tillotston. Billy Dobbs, a lifelong Atlantan and professional hairstylist, was active in the Georgia Hairdressers and Cosmetologists Association. During the 1950s, his parents, Guy and Emily, had many friends in the entertainment field, including Mary Ellen Tillotston, who, under the stage name of Kalantan, was one of the most popular exotic dancers of the era.

WILLIAM DEVEAUX WILSON, 1953. After William Deveaux Wilson met Jack Strouss in Atlanta in the early 1950s, they dated exclusively for almost two years. Wilson's parents owned a mobile home retail business based in Augusta. In 1953, the Wilson family moved to Dallas, Texas, and Jack and William wrote poignant letters to one another for a short time. They never saw each other again.

DOUGLAS JOHNSON AND WILLIAM WEAVER, C. 1964. Douglas Johnson (left) and William Weaver (fourth from left) were members of the American Guild of Organists. In the Atlanta chapter, Johnson served as treasurer and Weaver as dean. They first met in 1947 while attending the University of Florida, where they both participated in an organ recital. At the reception that followed, Johnson's family brought a watermelon. Weaver remembered the occasion fondly, noting on the program next to Johnson's name, "The boy who brought the watermelon." Over the next six years, the two developed a close friendship that eventually became intimate. After moving to Atlanta, Johnson became a professor of pharmacology at the University of Georgia, and Weaver worked as an organist-choirmaster at St. Anne's Episcopal Church. The couple moved in together, first in a garage apartment in Midtown Atlanta. Using Johnson's GI Bill, they later bought a house together in Decatur.

BARBARA VOGEL, 1957. Born in 1939, Barbara Vogel grew up and attended school in Atlanta. She worked at Oxford Industries before starting a career at Grady Hospital that would span 36 years. Through a mutual friend, Vogel met Charlene McLemore. Both were in relationships with other women, but they eventually became romantically involved seven years later.

CHARLENE MCLEMORE, TENNESSEE, 1965. Charlene McLemore, born in 1946, was raised in the Smoky Mountains of Kingsport, Tennessee. In 1965, she married a Pentecostal minister and had two sons. When the relationship became abusive, McLemore divorced and began supporting the family. Years later, she met Barbara Vogel, and the two began a friendship that would culminate in a life partnership.

SOUVENIR PROGRAM

17th ANNIVERSARY

ATLANTA TOMBOYS

1944 – 1960

SOFTBALL AND BASKETBALL

TOMBOYS PROGRAM, 1960. Many women formed friendships and romantic relationships through softball teams like the Tomboys and the Lorelei Ladies. This sphere, however, was not exclusively occupied by lesbians and therefore required careful judgment and caution in coming out. Nonetheless, recreational sports in Atlanta, as in other cities of comparable size, provided an important space for women to socialize with one another. Barbara Vogel reminisced, "They [the Lorelei Ladies and Tomboys] were significant teams, and they were heavily in the center of the gay life in Atlanta at that time. So if you were going to be in with the group, you followed the softball teams."

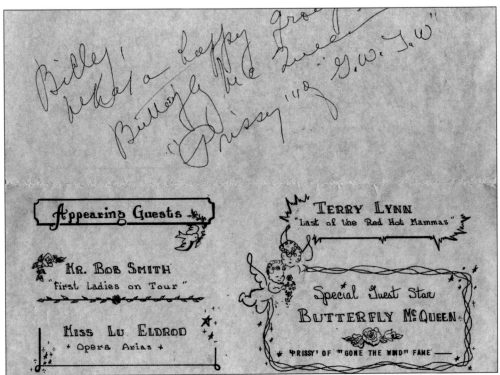

Billy!
What a happy gro[up]
Butterfly McQueen
"Prissy" '40 "G.W.T.W"

Appearing Guests

Mr. Bob Smith
"First Ladies on Tour"

Miss Lu Elrod
+ Opera Arias +

Terry Lynn
"Last of the Red Hot Mammas"

Special Guest Star
Butterfly McQueen
"PRISSY" OF "GONE THE WIND" FAME

HOUSE PARTY AND INVITATION, C. 1964. Annual parties celebrating national holidays or signature events, such as the Sarah Siddon Awards in Savannah, filled lesbian and gay social calendars and facilitated the expansion of social networks. On May 16, 1964, Billy Jones and Cliff Lietch hosted a Spring Festival. Its featured guests included Bob Smith, "First Ladies on Tour"; "Miss Lu Elrod, singing an opera aria"; Terry Lynn, "Last of the Red Hot Mammas"; and special guest star Butterfly McQueen, who played Prissy in the film *Gone With the Wind*. On the invitation, McQueen inscribed to Billy Jones, "What a happy group! Butterfly McQueen, 'Prissy' of 'GWTW.'"

54

DIAMOND LIL. Born in Savannah, Phillip Forrester moved to Atlanta and began his career as Diamond Lil in the 1960s, performing at numerous gay venues. During this time, Lil also wrote for *The Great Speckled Bird*, a local underground newspaper. Diamond Lil continues to perform in Atlanta.

JOY LOUNGE, 1968. The Joy Lounge opened on Ponce de Leon Avenue near Mrs. P's around 1967. Dupree's was located two blocks away on Ponce. These bars were among the first in the city to cater exclusively to gays and lesbians. After years of meeting in groups at various bars, restaurants, and hotels, mostly downtown, lesbian and gay Atlantans claimed public space for themselves in the 1960s.

FREDDIE STYLES AND HIS MOTHER, ANNIE, 1969. During the 1960s, Freddie Styles participated in the Atlanta University Annual Exhibition, established by artist and educator Hale Woodruff. Begun in 1942, the exhibition was a juried national competition for new and established African American artists. In 1969, Styles was awarded second place in the Graphics category. (Courtesy Clark Atlanta University Art Galleries.)

LA CAROUSEL LOUNGE, C. 1960. At 834 Hunter Street (now Martin Luther King Jr. Drive), La Carousel stood adjacent to Paschal's, a well-known restaurant founded and run by two African American brothers, James and Robert Paschal. La Carousel was a jazz club offering one of the city's few venues for cross-race socializing. It also attracted a gay and lesbian clientele.

Daytona, Florida, 1969 (right); New Orleans, Louisiana, 1969 (below). The social networks of Atlanta's gays and lesbians extended to nearby cities such as Birmingham, Alabama; Chattanooga, Tennessee; and Savannah, Georgia. For those who were financially able, travel beyond the Southeast was also an important shared outlet. Enhancing these networks were the new destination guides about gay and lesbian gathering places in cities across the country. *The International Guild Guide* for 1969 includes hotels, lounges, restaurants, and taverns for the Georgia cities of Albany, Atlanta, Augusta, Macon, and Savannah. Atlanta listings included the Blue Room in the Americana Motel and the Cameo Lounge on Spring Street; Dupree's Lounge and Restaurant, Joy Lounge, and Mrs. P's on Ponce de Leon; the Club South Baths; the Riviera Motel and the Piccolo Lounge on Peachtree Street; the Prince George Inn; and Wit's End.

BILLY JONES (STANDING, RIGHT) AND FRIENDS, PENSACOLA BEACH, FLORIDA, 1968. In the late 1950s, a small group of gay men in Florida began hosting Emma Jones parties. The name came from a pseudonym adopted by men to avoid prosecution from the U.S. Postal Service when receiving banned materials through the mail. By the early 1970s, the now-annual Fourth of July celebration at Pensacola Beach was drawing nearly 2,000 attendees.

EMMA JONES INVITATION, 1970. In 1970, Ray and Henry and Pete and Wayne, two couples hosting the event, sent invitations reading, "It's the age of Aquarius and to all those adventurous, we shall meet again at last in the sands for a blast! George and Abe liked this time, for it gave them reason and rhyme. You will need a car or gondola; so 'Let's get together in Pensacola.'"

Three

PARTIES, POLITICS, AND PRIDE

1970–1990

The Stonewall Inn riots in Greenwich Village in New York in the summer of 1969 were a significant event in the struggle for gay and lesbian equality. In the early 21st century, Stonewall continues to hold symbolism for lesbian, gay, bisexual, and transgender (LGBT) activists. Most historians agree that it separates the post–World War II assimilationist homophile movement from the era of gay liberation, gay pride, and diverse sexual and gender radical movements that followed.

In Atlanta, as elsewhere, the Stonewall riots inspired a small group of gays and lesbians to organize. Atlantans began commemorating Stonewall in gay pride marches, formed a chapter of the national Gay Liberation Front, and, within a few years, created dozens of religious, political, and cultural groups ranging from lesbian feminist organizations, to theater troupes, to synagogues. Each laid claim to dignity and equality.

As liberationist movements unfolded in Atlanta in the early 1970s, they often overlapped and intertwined with the explosion of bars, restaurants, lounges, bookstores, centers, and sports and recreation teams catering to lesbians and gays. Many of the bars sponsored teams, hosted fund-raisers and political and religious events, and featured drag shows that mixed ribald humor with wry political commentary. The line between socializing and politics blurred during the 1970s. The notion of pride—whether expressed in a rally at Piedmont Park or onstage at the Sweet Gum Head—was both a celebration and a political expression.

The popularity of bars and parties did not wane in the 1980s, but the gay social and political landscape of Atlanta, as in other major cities, was transformed by the AIDS crisis. Much, though not all, activism during the decade centered on AIDS, and lesbians played an important role in the movement to educate people and to combat the increasingly vocal anti-gay forces from the Christian right and the Republican Party.

DAVID, 1971. The map (pictured left) and accompanying guide to "Cruising Atlanta" appeared in *David*, a monthly gay magazine that began publication in Jacksonville, Florida, in December 1970. Its purpose, articulated in the inaugural issue, was to "report on the news of special interest for the Southeastern homophile community." It also included detailed information about bars, clubs, and other gay destinations. By 1971, Mrs. P's remained popular but was now joined by many bars that had opened in the late 1960s, most of which were clustered in Midtown and along Ponce de Leon. In addition to bars, other gay-specific entertainment venues became popular during this period, including bookstores, adult theaters, and baths. As *David* advised, "Be careful, though. Once you taste Atlanta's brand of Southern hospitality, you may never want to leave."

GAY ATLANTA

1. ANSLEY MALL FLORIST
2. THE ARMORY
3. MR. B'S BOOK STORE
4. CLUB SOUTH BATHS
5. THE COVE
6. FUNOCHIO'S
7. GAY PAREE CINEMA
8. MRS. P'S
9. ONYX LOUNGE
10. OTHER ROOM RESTAURANT
11. PEACHES BACK DOOR
12. PICADILLY LOUNGE
13. THE RATHSKELLER
14. SWEET GUM HEAD

Be careful though. Once you taste Atlanta's brand of Southern hospitality, you may never want to leave.

REVOLUTIONARY

Gay Flames
Pamphlet
No. 11

10¢

AN INTRODUCTION TO GAY LIBERATION

By Guy Nassberg

Homosexuals are an oppressed minority in American society. America has forced us -- I speak particularly of male homosexuals, because I am one -- into urban ghettos, almost the only place where we can find one another, and into the few jobs and professions where we can get by. We meet in dimly-lit dehumanizing gay bars; at private parties; or on the streets, where we have been beaten and murdered, and arrested by plainclothes pigs who entrap us. Often, we never meet, struggling with the "burden" of our homosexuality in isolated despair, committing suicide or dying as prisoners in mental hospitals. If we do come out to each other, most of us are compelled to lead double lives, at the cost of loss of jobs, housing, and contact with a vast portion of the human race.

We hide and torment ourselves because this society says we are "sick," and to varying degrees we believe it. America allows us to live only one way, in penance and shame for our "unnatural" natures. Accepting in one way or another what America says about us, we feel powerless to fight, and become slaves of what straight society calls our unchangable "human nature."

The Gay Liberation Front (GLF) has been formed all across the country to fight the enslaving lies and myths which America hopes to perpetuate. We are following the example of the Third World and Women's Liberation movements in rejecting what we are told we must be, and fighting for an alternative to this oppressive society. We know that we are not sick. Beyong all the Freudian rot about our mothers and fathers, and the phony masculine myths about our inadequacies, lies something that bullshit theories can't explain away: we like making love with people of the same sex. We feel good and whole making love. We want to remain homosexual.

Homosexuality is the ability to relate sexually and spiritually to someone of the same sex. Human beings need to unite with other human beings, and homosexuals unite with people who have the same genitals. That's a great thing, and we who are homosexual, and groove on each other, have nothing to hide or escape.

People who are petrified of us (especially men), and who put us down, are off the wall. The only thing that is wrong with us is that America won't let us feel right in doing what we must do. America makes homosexuality our problem, and its problem, when homosexuality could be the basis of our pleasure and fulfillment. It is time for us to straighten out straight society.

All human relationships are a mess in America. What else can you expect in a capitalist system? America has everyone competing with each other, put-

REVOLUTIONARY LOVE PAMPHLET, C. 1971. The Stonewall riots of 1969 inspired the formation of political activist organizations in New York and other major cities. The largest was the Gay Liberation Front, founded in 1970, which in turn gave a name to this new brand of lesbian and gay activism as a minority group demanding equal rights, respect, and freedom from religious, social, and legal repression: the gay liberation movement. This pamphlet, one of many in the possession of James Kambourian, a member of the Committee on Gay Education at the University of Georgia in the early 1970s, exemplifies the proliferation of gay liberation groups across the country. In 1970, Miami, Florida, transplant Berl Boykin organized a rally in Piedmont Park to commemorate the anniversary of the Stonewall riots. The following year, Atlanta activists established a local chapter of the Gay Liberation Front.

CLUB CENTAUR POSTER, 1970. Club Centaur opened on the corner of Peachtree and Eleventh Streets in May 1970. It closed in November of the same year. During those six months, however, it became well known for its outrageous drag shows backed by a live band and featuring performers like Diamond Lil and Phyllis Killer. The November 1, 1970, issue of the countercultural newspaper *The Great Speckled Bird* described the scene: "The crowds are younger, freakier, louder, hipper and a lot more fun to be with than what you might have imagined—Atlanta's coming out, to say the least!" If the city was "coming out," it was still a risky proposition, particularly as far as the Atlanta police were concerned, or as *The Great Speckled Bird* called them, "the uniformed pigs who traipse in and out, off and on, and who keep you aware that just a shot and a kiss away from the stage, the lights, the gowns, the music and the make-up, there is a new world busy being born and a pitiful, helpless old world busy dying."

INMAN "BUDDY" CLARK AND MICKY DAY, 1974. Buddy Clark (left) was born in Decatur in 1943. During a two-year stint in the army, Clark, a champion baton twirler, won the army's Best Entertainer Award and began performing at posts up and down the East Coast. After his discharge in 1966, he parlayed twirling into drag performing in a popular group called the Sir-Premes, which toured the Southeast during the late 1960s. Clark was diagnosed with AIDS in 1984, became an activist, and died in 1992 at the age of 49. Micky Day, born Michael Mellene, began his career as a female impersonator in Indianapolis, Indiana, and moved to Atlanta in 1972. Day became a regular performer and later the show director at the popular Onyx Club, a gay bar on West Peachtree Street in downtown Atlanta.

HOUSE PARTIES, c. 1971. The late 1960s and early 1970s witnessed an explosion of new forms and expressions of youth culture. From hippies and yippies, to Black Panthers and women's liberationists, many young people cast off what they saw as the confining middle-class strictures of their parents' generation or openly rebelled against what appeared to them as hypocritical and oppressive rules. The same was true for many young gays and lesbians, who embraced their identities in new, more public ways than had previous generations. In Atlanta, gay liberation and feminism served as vehicles for younger people to express these identities.

PIEDMONT PARK, 1971. Midtown and Little Five Points became the focal points of gay and lesbian life in Atlanta by the mid-1970s. In 1976, Richard Kavanaugh (center) launched *Cruise* magazine, a monthly guide to the city's gay bars and social activities.

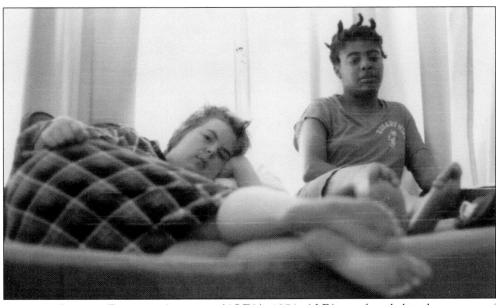

ATLANTA LESBIAN FEMINIST ALLIANCE (ALFA), 1974. ALFA was founded in the summer of 1972; the group's meeting place, ALFA House, was located on McLendon Avenue near Little Five Points. The following year, ALFA participated in the annual commemoration of Stonewall in Piedmont Park. In 1974, the group fielded the city's first all-lesbian softball team, established consciousness-raising (or "rap") groups, and hosted Rita Mae Brown reading from her novel *Rubyfruit Jungle*.

WOMANSONG THEATER, 1974. Pam Parker (second from left), along with fellow members of ALFA and other lesbian feminists, participated in musical groups like WomanSong and organized political and social gatherings, often held in Piedmont Park, in support of the ratification of the Equal Rights Amendment (ERA).

ERA PICNIC, 1975. In Atlanta, as elsewhere during the 1970s, women's sexual identity was often intertwined with feminist consciousness. Lesbian feminists played an important and visible role within the larger women's movement, and they were skilled at combining political critique with their own unique brand of cultural expression, whether through music, poetry and writing, theater, or art.

Jeanne Aland and Fran Pici, 1975. Fran Pici (right) was a cofounder of Red Dyke Theatre (RDT), established in 1974 by a group of Atlanta lesbians, who were self-described as sharing an interest in "theatre, dancing and boogying, lesbian/feminist politics, and huge egos!" who had grown weary of what they called "male-identified theatre." They sought new forms of entertainment beyond gay bars, disco music, and drag shows. "The members of RDT were very involved in both the gay and lesbian and women's communities," Pici explained. "We developed an appreciation and formed a kinship with the 'drag queens'" whom the Red Dyke Theatre members "chose to parody" in their early performances. RDT's first show was a benefit for ALFA softball teams. Soon, as the company gained popularity in some of Atlanta's most popular gay bars like the Tower Lounge and the Sweet Gum Head, its shows became more elaborate. Performers expanded their original parodies into skits and experimental theater that tackled more serious issues facing women and lesbians, and incorporated music, photography, and film into their shows.

LORELEI LADIES, 1975. One of the hallmarks of post–World War II lesbian culture was the organized softball league. Atlanta's Lorelei Ladies, founded in 1939, proved especially appealing to lesbians with a keen interest in sports. As a 1968 souvenir booklet pointed out, "No renumeration [*sic*] is given any member of the Lorelei Ladies for playing ball; they play for the love of the sport and for the physical, mental, and social benefits derived from it."

PAM PARKER, SIXTH MICHIGAN WOMYN'S FESTIVAL, 1981. Pam Parker was born in 1955 and grew up in the Cabbagetown neighborhood of Atlanta, a working-class district surrounding the Fulton bag and cotton mills. She began her creative career as a singer-songwriter and, in the 1980s and 1990s, became a playwright. Among Parker's best known works are *Special Pals*, *Second Samuel*, and *Grass Windows*, which was produced off-Broadway in 1991.

GIL ROBISON, C. 1980. Gil Robison was among the founders of Atlanta's first gay political action committee, the First Tuesday Democratic Club, which was established in July 1977. The organizers chose the name to commemorate the day the Miami-Dade County City Council passed a human rights ordinance including lesbians and gays. The referendum held great symbolic power for activists outside of Florida. First Tuesday began lobbying and voter registration efforts in Atlanta.

FRANK SCHEUREN, 1977. Frank Scheuren served as the national president of the Catholic gay rights organization Dignity Incorporated, which started in San Diego, California, as a support group for gays and lesbians. A well-known activist in Atlanta in the late 1970s and early 1980s, Scheuren was also the first chair of the Atlanta Gay Center Board and cochair of the Gay Rights National Lobby.

Atlanta Barb

"THE GROOVY NEWSPAPER SERVING ATLANTA AND NEIGHBORING CITIES"

VOL. 1 NO. 1   **OVER 5,000 IN CIRCULATION**   **25 CENTS**

Peral Bailee
Entertainer of The Month Atlanta's Own

Mr. Peral Bailee Takes Atlanta By Storm!

An interview with Mr. Peral Bailee, is a most interesting and rewarding experience. Originally from Atlanta, our Peral has been a professional female impersonator for 7 years. He has graced the stage of every gay lounge in Atlanta that has presented shows. Of course, his carêer has branched out to performances in Augusta, Alabama, North Carolina, Florida and Kentucky.

His talent is dynamic, and his wardrobe resembles that of a real super star. When questioned about the real Pearl Bailey, he said, "She is fabulous and she's my idol". It's no wonder he was thrilled when he actually met the real Pearl Bailey in person.

Although he has no intention of having a full time career in the entertainment field, Peral has definite convictions concerning the art of female impersonation. "You must have a talent for it. A person must take the time to do their work well. When I do Pearl, I'm not doing her, I'm doing myself "naturally" replied Peral seriously.

Continued on Back Cover

✦ OPEN LETTER TO THE READERS ✦

Thank you . . . Fine Readers,

For all the response in supporting the Atlanta Barb. We are very pleased with the cooperation we received from our Lounges, and other advertisers who have helped this much needed publication make a success.

Our special thanks to all those involved with the Metropolitan Community Churches throughout the country, for supporting and distributing the newspaper.

In order for us to bring to you news and events that hold your interest, please write to us offering any suggestions, or comments. We welcome criticism as well as advice. This is your newspaper and the success will depend upon you.

Our entertainer of the Month will be chosen by you the reader, as well as the Bartender, and the Stud of the Month. You now have an opportunity to "Speak your Peace," So let me hear from you.

The Editor

OUR VALENTINE, ALLISON

Blonde Bombshell Of Drag

"Try it, you'll like it, should be this blonde bombshell's motto. Mr. Allison radiates glamour and sex appeal, just as sure as the moon was made for lovers. He has appeared "just about everywhere, every big name club in town." If you have seen his action packed performance, you will understand why. Allison knows how to "drive audiences wild" and he enjoys every minute of it.

Being considered a "Super Star" and a "natural male actress" is a feat in itself

and Allison has certainly accomplished this.

He is currently working at the "number one Show Bar" of Atlanta, the Sweet Gum Head, but must be ready by the beginning of summer to return to his own show. This show appropriately named the "Misfits," consists of five star performers, and has appeared all over the North East. from Alantic City, N.J. to Maine. Allison's whole life seems to revolve

around "show business",, therefore he has little time to pursue any other interestsi or hobbys. He does have an adorable little mini collie named "Sadie", who travels with him, that he loves dearly (lucky dog) Allison was first runner up in the first "Miss Gay Atlanta" pageant, but isn't interested in entering any others (that's their loss) . He has attended the University of Georgia (drama) and is a native of Athens Ga... Zodiac sign - Would you believe a Capricorn?????

Atlanta Barb   **P.O. Box 82543 Atlanta, Georgia 30354**   **Phone 363-4789**

ATLANTA BARB, **1974.** Bill Smith, a leading gay activist in the 1970s, founded Atlanta's first gay newspaper, later named the *Barb,* in 1974. Unlike other local or regional publications, it focused on events, politics, and issues that affected lesbians and gays in Atlanta rather than serving strictly as a guide to bars and clubs. The following year, at the building Smith owned on West Peachtree and Fourth Streets, an informal gay community group began meeting. It later became the Atlanta Gay Center, but during its first year, it featured discussion groups, a meeting space, and a telephone hotline.

CRUISE, 1976. As the founding editors of *Cruise* noted in the inaugural issue of January 1976 (right), "The gay population and the number of businesses that cater to them have experienced an explosive growth in the last few years. New clubs are opening every month, old ones are changing their format," and Atlanta's lesbians and gays were frequenting them enthusiastically. In this ever-changing landscape of gay nightlife, *Cruise* promised to "provide an up-to-date Guide to all of those bars, restaurants, lounges, discos, baths, cinemas, book stores and other places of entertainment that welcome the gay crowd." The publishers quickly learned that the busy lesbian and gay social schedule necessitated putting out a weekly supplement. The first free *Cruise* calendar (below) was published in August 1976.

January 1976/$1.00

CRUISE

THE ENTERTAINMENT GUIDE TO GAY ATLANTA

Volume 1/No. 1   August 6 through August 12, 1976

CRUISE
Weekly Calendar

FREE

FRANK POWELL AND CHUCK CAIN, C. 1975. Two major gay bar entrepreneurs were Frank Powell (left) and Chuck Cain. Over the years, Powell owned more than a dozen bars, including Payton Place, which featured a drag comedy revue starring Phyllis Killer. Cain is perhaps best remembered for Chuck's Rathskeller, a gay night club.

NINTH ANNUAL PHYLLIS KILLER OSCAR AWARDS, 1977. Although originally created in a lighthearted spirit, Billy Jones's signature annual event, the Phyllis Killer Oscar Awards, became a serious effort to honor bar and business owners, as well as all the men and women onstage and behind the scenes, from the 1970s to the mid-1980s.

MISS AND MR. GAY ATLANTA PAGEANTS, 1977 AND 1975. On Halloween night in 1970, Buddy Clark staged the first Miss Gay Atlanta Pageant at the Rathskeller. From the beginning, the pageant was a local favorite, and in 1975, it was moved to the first week of June because, in Clark's words, it had become a "gala event which required a night of its own." After the Rathskeller closed in 1972, Miss Gay Atlanta moved to the Sweet Gum Head (pictured above). In 1979, the pageant celebrated its 10th anniversary and created a board of directors, increased the prize money, and became an Atlanta institution for the next 30 years. Beginning in 1975, the Mr. Gay Atlanta Pageant featured men in evening wear, casual wear, and white bikinis (pictured below).

BACKSTREET, C. 1975. The place that would become known as Backstreet, recognized by the round white sign bearing a black cat (upper right), began as Peaches Back Room in 1971, touting itself as the "newest, finest, plushest, and grooviest club in Atlanta." It was located in the heart of Midtown at 845 Peachtree Street in the back room of Joe's Disco. The bar, which had its own entrance, started and ended as a private club, defined by the State of Georgia as an organization with a minimum of 250 dues-paying members. For close to three decades, Backstreet was "open and pouring," one of the few 24-hour nightclubs in the city. As Midtown gentrified in the late 1990s, what was once considered a marker of a large, modern, and cosmopolitan city—24-hour nightlife—ended by New Year's Eve 2003 when private clubs were forced to shut their doors as new closing hours for the city's nightclubs and bars went into effect.

THE PRINCE GEORGE INN, C. 1978. Located at Sixth and Juniper Streets in Midtown, the Prince George Inn was a popular lounge and restaurant catering to a mixed clientele. The business was originally owned by Charles Cain and William Copeland in the mid-1960s, and Copeland became the sole owner in the 1970s. Located near the Armory and Backstreet, it was an integral part of the gay social scene, with facilities to also accommodate the functions of social and religious groups.

SHELLY'S PLACE, 1978. In an office building at Peachtree and Twenty-fifth Streets, north of Midtown, Shelly's Place was a gay restaurant and disco. In a previous incarnation, it had been called the Smugglers Inn, a bar and restaurant aimed at the straight business crowd. Owned and operated by Allen Jones and two business partners, the popular spot became known for its Sunday brunch and tea dance.

PERSHING POINT HOTEL, 1977.
The hotel, situated on the northern
end of Midtown, was home to an
assortment of artists, writers, hippies,
drag queens, and gay men and women
during the 1970s. Some likened it
to the Chelsea Hotel in Manhattan
or San Francisco's Haight-Ashbury
District. Gay actor Leslie Jordan, best
known for his role on the sitcom *Will
and Grace*, lived here in 1974.

PEACHTREE MANOR HOTEL, 1977.
Renowned Atlanta architect J. Neel
Reid designed this hotel, which was
built on Peachtree Street in the
heart of Midtown in 1924. In 1962,
it became one of the first hotels in
the South to integrate voluntarily,
and by the early 1970s, it was
the site of businesses catering to
Atlanta's emerging gay community.

GALLUS RESTAURANT AND LOUNGE, 1977. Opened in the mid-1970s, Gallus, a restaurant and tavern on Sixth Street in Midtown, was a focal point of the city's gay nightlife. Its downstairs lounge featured Mabel the piano player for several years. Until it was destroyed by a fire in the early 1990s, the Gallus thrived, as did other restaurants and lounges, especially ones with live entertainment, including Gene and Gabe's Restaurant. When it opened at 1578 Piedmont Road in 1965, Gene and Gabe's Restaurant quickly became the city's "in" restaurant. In the national guidebook *The Gay Insider USA*, published in 1972, John Francis Hunter recalled a memorable moment there: "Gene [Dale] was in a review with Joan Rivers in Falmouth when I was working the other end of the Cape with another unknown, Ruth Buzzi. And who should saunter into G and G's the very night of my visit but Ms. Buzzi herself." Gene Dale and Gabe Bencivenga were known for providing the best in cabaret entertainment and accommodating facilities for social functions and private affairs.

PROTESTERS, C. 1977. When Miami-Dade County passed a gay rights ordinance in 1977, Anita Bryant, a beauty queen and Florida orange juice spokesperson, emerged as the leader of the fight to repeal the legislation. The Save Our Children campaign, carried out by fundamentalist Christians and social conservatives, became a flash point in the emerging culture war, energizing activists on both the right and the left across the country. In Atlanta, activists organized orange juice boycotts and invoked Bryant's name and face in pride marches and public protests. In an editorial in the *Barb*, Bill Smith urged readers to contact the Florida Citrus Commission and "let them know that as long as Ms. Bryant is their choice for 'Orange Queen' you won't be buying their product." Many conservative supporters later spurned Bryant when she divorced her husband, Bob Green, in 1980.

GAY PRIDE, 1977. In the summer of 1977, Atlanta mayor Maynard Jackson issued a proclamation for Civil Liberties Day rather than Gay Pride Day, which he had supported the year before. This name change was intended to appease a vocal group of religious conservatives, most notably a group called Citizens for Decency. Gay Pride Week organizers Linda Reigner and Victor Host responded with outrage. The reactions of lesbians and gays in Atlanta were characterized in an August 1977 article in the *Barb* as ranging from "disappointment to anger." In the same issue, Larry Laughlin penned the article "Gay Pride March Is Very Moving Experience" after attending his first demonstration for a "political reason." "From the moment the *Barb* mobile arrived at the Civic Center I knew I was in for a high. People—lots of people—gathered to march for gay rights and gay pride." He concluded, "If the March did nothing else but show other gays our potential, it was well worth the effort."

REV. TROY PERRY, C. 1979. Along with a dozen other men and women, Troy Perry founded the Universal Fellowship of Metropolitan Community Churches in Los Angeles, California, in 1968. Perry was a former Pentecostal pastor who recognized the growing need to address gays' and lesbians' feelings of exclusion from and isolation within organized religion. The movement grew, and in 1972, Atlanta established its own Metropolitan Community Church.

METROPOLITAN COMMUNITY CHURCH, 1981. Within months of forming, the Metropolitan Community Church found its first permanent home on Highland Avenue in the Virginia Highland neighborhood east of Midtown. Rev. John Gill of Pennsylvania served as its founding pastor. By the 1990s, after the church had moved farther north of its original location, weekly attendance was ranging from 300 to 400. It remains an important community institution.

LUTHERANS CONCERNED, 1979. This meeting, which was held in February 1979 at the Prince George Inn, marked the fourth anniversary of the founding of the Atlanta chapter of Lutherans Concerned. In addition to the Metropolitan Community Church and Lutherans Concerned, Atlanta was home to many other gay religious organizations that began in the 1970s and early 1980s.

BRIDGES, NOVEMBER 1981. The nondenominational Christian group Evangelical Outreach Ministries was one of the many religious groups formed during the 1970s and 1980s. Others included Dignity Atlanta (for Catholics), Integrity Atlanta (for Episcopalians), and the Jewish Congregation Bet Haverim. For lesbians and gays of faith, these organizations provided mutual support and a means to challenge discrimination.

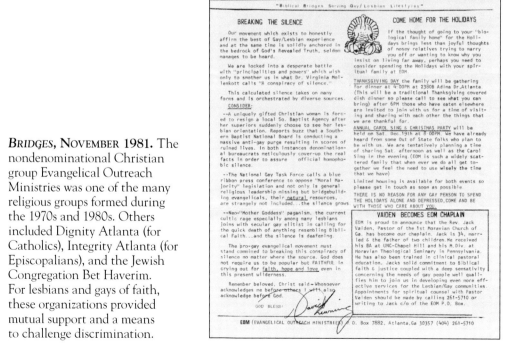

THE BUFFALO CHIPS, C. 1982. The Buffalo Chips were an all-male, gay clogging group that performed at the World's Fair in 1982 in Knoxville, Tennessee, and at the International Mr. Leather Contest in Chicago. The group was one of many sponsored by Atlanta Venture Sports, a nonprofit organization devoted to meeting the social, recreational, and educational needs of Atlanta's gay and lesbian communities. Members appear onstage at Illusions (pictured above).

HOTLANTA RIVER EXPO, C. 1981. In 1978, this annual event began with 300 gay men rafting down a section of the Chattahoochee River. Within a decade, its name had changed to the Hotlanta River Expo, and it had grown into one of the largest and most popular gay events in the Southeast. The daylong rafting festival expanded into four days of parties incorporating such performances as the Mr. and Miss Hotlanta Pageants.

ATLANTA BUSINESS AND PROFESSIONAL GUILD ADVERTISEMENT, 1985. The guild was established in 1978 to bring together gay business and professional men and women. It supported community activities, sponsored programs and special events, and published a monthly newspaper and an annual business directory. The guild was a sign of the growing economic power of gays and lesbians and their claim to a visible presence within the marketplace.

BOARD OF FIRST TUESDAY, C. 1981. In 1977, a group of lesbians and gays established the city's first gay political action committee, which by 1980 would be known as the First Tuesday Association for Lesbian and Gay Rights. According to the group's constitution, First Tuesday was formed to "create an awareness that gay people should be fully and equally represented in the local and national body politic."

ATLANTA GAY CENTER, C. 1980. The Atlanta Gay Center moved from its original location on West Peachtree Street to Ponce de Leon Avenue in 1980. As gay entertainment venues, religious groups, and business and social networking organizations continued to proliferate in the late 1970s and early 1980s, the Atlanta Gay Center needed additional space. In 1981, after this photograph was taken, the facility added a wheelchair ramp to the front entrance to increase accessibility.

CHRISTOPHER'S KIND BOOKSELLER, 1980. In June 1980, Christopher's Kind Bookseller opened in the Atlanta Gay Center. It specialized in the growing body of literature in gay and lesbian studies, fiction and poetry, travel, spirituality, and other genres. Christopher's Kind followed in the footsteps of Charis Books and More, an independent feminist bookstore that opened in Little Five Points in 1974 and included books aimed at lesbian readers.

MARÍA HELENA DOLAN, C. 1982. Dolan (right) was a major figure in Atlanta's feminist and gay and lesbian communities beginning in the late 1970s. She worked as an organizer for the 1979 and 1987 Marches on Washington and for numerous gay pride events. Combining irreverence with passionate activism, Dolan was a founding member of the feminist theater troupe Mother of the Sisters of No Mercy and Southern Ladies Against Women (SLAW).

DAVID HAYWARD AND FRIENDS, C. 1981. A community activist during the 1970s and 1980s, David Hayward (left)—shown with Gil Robison (center) and an unidentified person—frequently wrote for gay and lesbian publications, including the *Gazette* newspaper. He was also involved with local gay film festivals. Hayward brought gay activism to Atlanta's airwaves on Georgia Tech's WREK in 1972 and through "Gay Digest," a program that aired on WRFG in the late 1970s.

ATLANTANS AT THE MARCH ON WASHINGTON, D.C., 1979. John Howell (pictured above, second from left) served as president of the Virginia Highland Neighborhood Association and actively participated in the Georgia AIDS Action Council, Legislate Equality for Gays and Lesbians (LEGAL), and Southeastern Arts, Media, and Education (SAME). Following his death from HIV-related complications in 1988, the John Howell Park on Virginia Avenue was dedicated to his memory. The first national March on Washington for gay and lesbian equality took place on October 14, 1979. It was organized in response to several high-profile events, including the assassination of openly gay San Francisco city supervisor Harvey Milk and Anita Bryant's Save Our Children campaign. It also marked the 10th anniversary of the Stonewall uprising and demonstrated the powerful symbolism of community.

LESBIAN, GAY, AND TRANSPERSON PRIDE RALLY, 1980. In 1971, an estimated 125 to 150 people attended the first permit-authorized event; by 1980, the number had grown to nearly 1,200, and that number had quadrupled by 1990. Throughout the 1970s and 1980s, Atlantans participated in efforts to foster a national gay identity. In the 1986 Pride Guide festival souvenir program, María Helena Dolan wrote, "June is Pride month. The time when it is most appropriate to be defiant, to feel our collective strength, to revel in the sense of community. It's our Bastile [sic] Day. Please, celebrate and nurture that spirit during Pride week—and all year." As a sign of the growing and diversifying community, in 1980, organizers changed the name of Gay Pride Day to Lesbian, Gay, and Transperson Pride Day. The word transperson was dropped from the name after 1980.

STAFF OF THE SWEET GUM HEAD, C. 1980. This bar on Cheshire Bridge Road (by the late 1970s known as "the Great Gay Way") opened in 1971 and was operated by Chuck Cain and Frank Powell. Billed as "the place for the 'now' generation," it was known for its drag shows. It also hosted community events and fund-raisers. The Sweet Gum Head closed in 1981 and was replaced by a heterosexual strip club.

CHARLIE BROWN, 1979. Born in Tennessee, Charlie Brown first made his name as a female impersonator in the Miss Midwest Pageant in Newport, Kentucky. After moving to Atlanta in 1973, he became a regular hostess and performer at the Sweet Gum Head. His career flourished for the next three decades.

Texas Drilling Company, 1981. Located at 1026½ North Highland Avenue in the heart of the Virginia Highland neighborhood, the Texas Drilling Company catered to the "leather-levi" crowd, one of the many subcultures that proliferated during this period. In 1979, ten gay men founded the Leathermen of Atlanta. Their fourth anniversary program notes that in 1981 and 1982 the organization "joined ranks with Atlantis M. C., the Saddletramps and the Georgia Brigade and presented the Atlanta 4-Way."

Illusions, c. 1982. Tony DeSario (left), Ted Binkley (center), and Randy Sullivan are pictured in front of Illusions on Peachtree Street. Ted Binkley and Ray Ferris co-owned Crazy Ray'z on Piedmont Road and Illusions. In 1982, just after the Sweet Gum Head had closed, Illusions borrowed its old tag line as the "Show Place of the South." In 1985, Chaka Khan made a surprise appearance and performed her hit song "I Feel for You."

AID atlanta
♪♪♪ NEWSLETTER ♪♪♪

| vol. 1 no. 1 | 9 bi-monthly 8 3 | july/august |

FUNDRAISING - A COMMUNITY EFFORT

Susan Martin

Ray Kayman

While AID Atlanta has had to assume full responsibility for funding its activities and services, help from within the community has come from a variety of sources.

Ray Kayman, a cancer patient whose case was diagnosed as terminal ten years ago, has turned his fighting spirit to generating money for AIDS. Kayman has taken pledges of $5,310 in his bid to drop 50 pounds by August 31. Already lighter by 22 pounds, Kayman says his success was made easier by thinking of people with AIDS who are in a similar condition to his a few years ago. This "Diet for AIDS," which will end when Kayman is weighed in at the Ansley Kroger meat department on August 31, has been conducted under medical supervision.

Susan Martin also utilized her personal strength and physical stamina to raise money for AIDS. Ms. Martin not only ran in and successfully completed this year's Peachtree Road Race, but has also solicited over $3,000 in pledges – money which she has turned in to AID Atlanta.

Local bar owners and businesses have shown their support and community spirit in donating their proceeds to AID Atlanta from shows, parties, raffles, and receptions. We would like to thank Crazy Ray's for their Christmas Benefit, Redoubt for their Black Party and Christmas Party, The Royal Court of Atlanta for their fabulous show at Illusions, Corporate Promotions for their donation from the

Bride of Frankenstein Party, Form and Function Gallery for providing their artistic reception space, Bulldog's and Sunset People for their donations, and The Sportspage for their Benefit Fundraiser.

Recent fundraising events initiated by communities outside of Atlanta, such as Columbia, S.C. (Rumors), Chattanooga (Alan Gold's), and Savannah (Who's Who) are broadening our outreach. Funds raised outside of Atlanta by groups such as these and donated to AID Atlanta, are specifically slated for use in regional networking and for public information and service provision in those areas. With the recent formation of the National AIDS Federation, AID Atlanta, as Southeastern representative, has undertaken additional outreach to these communities. If you are interested in organizing a fundraiser in your area and would like to contact us for speakers, literature or resource information, call (404) 872-0600.

The Fundraising Committee of AID Atlanta indicates that there are a number of events in the planning stages. AIDS nights at local clubs, a Mardi Gras party, and movie nights have all been proposed, along with yard sales, a raffle, a six mile walk-a-thon, and a celebrity auction offering such items as a pack of cigarettes once owned by Bette Davis and Bruce Jenner's running shorts, going to the highest bidder.

A CALL TO ACTION

AID Atlanta is a totally volunteer organization established to educate and serve the Atlanta community, and to provide direct services and support for people with AIDS.

We would like to take this opportunity to thank you for the support you have given us. Individually, for your volunteer and financial support, and collectively, to the gay and lesbian business community which has come forth with both money and time to help us educate and support each other.

We would like to thank gay Atlanta entertainers who have so generously given their special talent to make our fundraisers successes.

We would like to thank the Atlanta press for professional and responsible journalism which has sought to inform and educate the community at large on the medical and social aspects of AIDS.

We stand face to face with an issue which has the potential of historically uniting us in a way we have never been united. In an unprecedented act of support, members of the Atlanta lesbian community came forward to organize and sponsor a benefit for AIDS. They offered as the slogan under which we marched to celebrate our gay pride: "AIDS — Together We Can Stop It." They recognized that although the medical aspects of the disease do not affect them, the political and social implications are terrifying to us all, and that together — gay, lesbian, heterosexual — concerned human beings, we can stop AIDS.

We use this opportunity not only to thank you for your past support but to issue a call to action.

We call on you to join us, for AID Atlanta is every concerned Atlantan. Join us in any way you can. Through active volunteer work, financial support, or in helping us spread accurate information about AIDS through positive networking with friends and work associates. We call on the Atlanta gay community to unite. For, no matter what our differences, it is because of our likeness that we will ultimately suffer.

We call for justice from our federal, state and local governments in the form of

Continued on Page 6

AID ATLANTA HOTLINE
INFORMATION AND REFERRAL
404-872-0600

AID CRISISLINE
NATIONAL GAY TASK FORCE
800-221-7044
Monday - Friday: 3pm - 9pm EST

AID ATLANTA NEWSLETTER, JULY–AUGUST 1983. AIDS first came to national attention in 1981. In Atlanta, thanks in part to the presence of the Centers for Disease Control, gay activists began organizing around the issue by 1983. AID Atlanta was an all-volunteer educational and service organization. This inaugural issue of the group's newsletter predicted that AIDS "has the potential of historically uniting us [lesbians and gays] in a way we have never been united."

THE NEWS, MAY 28, 1985. In 1982, Atlantan Michael Hardwick was arrested in his bedroom for engaging in oral sex with another man. Hardwick appealed, aided by the ACLU and Georgians Opposed to Archaic Laws. In 1986, the case reached the U.S. Supreme Court, which upheld Georgia's sodomy statute. The high court's 2003 ruling in *Lawrence v. Texas* overturned the sodomy law in Texas and, in turn, invalidated similar laws throughout the country.

A Publication of The Atlanta Gay Center

The News

Appeals Court Issues Decision in Hardwick Case

On May 21, the 11th U.S. Circuit Court of Appeals handed down its decision on the case involving Georgia's sodomy law. The appeals court failed to declare the law unconstitutional, but rather remanded the case back to the lower district court for trial.

In issuing the 2-to-1 ruling Justices Johnson and Tuttle said that "the Georgia sodomy statute infringes upon the fundamental constitutional rights of Michael Hardwick," and that the State "Must prove, in order to prevail, that it has a compelling interest" in regulating private sexual behavior.

Also in the ruling, Judge Johnson said "The intimate association protected against interference does not exist in the marriage relationship alone...For some, the sexual activity in question here serves the same purpose as the intimacy of marriage."

Judge Phyllis Kravitch said she didn't believe the court had the jurisdiction in the case otherwise she would rule with the majority.

The case was brought to trial by Michael Hardwick, who was arrested and charged with sodomy after an Atlanta police officer observed him having oral sex with a male partner, in the privacy of his bedroom. When the District Attorney decided to drop the case, Hardwick, assisted by the ACLU and GOAL, filed suit to challenge the law. Hardwick named State Attorney Mike Bowers, Fulton County District Attorney Lewis Slaton and Atlanta Public Safety Commissioner George Napper as defendants.

The case was thrown out of District court and was in appeal before the 11th Circuit Court of Appeals for over two years before they issued this ruling.

Calling the ruling a milestone, Kathleen Wilde, attorney for Hardwick said "This is

Center Finds New Home

After searching for nearly three months, the Atlanta Gay Center has found a new home at 63 Twelfth Street. The AGC looked at about 25 locations

made a move from an office building to a house in hopes of giving a more relaxed and comfortable atmosphere to the Center."

LAYTON GREGORY AND FRIENDS, C. 1983. Pictured from left to right are Dina Jacobs, Layton Gregory, Billy Jones, and Chena Black. Born in South Carolina in 1932, Gregory graduated from the Candler School of Theology at Emory, married, and had children. After 16 years, the couple divorced. Gregory served for years as a Methodist minister, but after his divorce, he had difficulty finding a church. Making a dramatic personal and professional turn, Gregory came out and invested in Club Atlanta (formerly Club South Baths), a popular Midtown gay bath on Fourth Street. He became co-owner in the 1970s. In a special dedication in the souvenir program of the 17th Annual Phyllis Killer Oscar Awards, Gregory's friend Billy Jones wrote, "In November 1984, on his deathbed, he [Gregory] made me promise I'd go on with the show, so with sadness in my heart and tears in my eyes, I say 'Layton, this one is for you. . . . Now let's go on with the show.'" It was the final year of the awards event.

GIL ROBISON AND MELVIN ROSS, C. 1983. Melvin Ross (right) was among several African American gay men who worked to promote racial tolerance within the gay community through such groups as Black and White Men Together, a national organization. The Atlanta chapter was founded in 1981. It published a newsletter, hosted potlucks and social outings, and sponsored programs like the Atlanta Anti-Discrimination Project 1983–1984, which challenged discriminatory entrance policies at local bars.

MR. GAMA PAGEANT, 1984. The Gay Atlanta Minority Association (GAMA) was founded in April 1979. A *Gazette* article from January 1981 noted that GAMA was created "as a result of complaints by a number of Third World persons regarding discrimination against them in some of Atlanta's gay bars and places of entertainment." On January 26, 1981, the first Mr. GAMA contest was held at the Sweet Gum Head and was hosted by Tina Devore (second row, far right).

Theo Thomas, Festival Lounge and Eatery, c. 1984. Theo Thomas served as the show director at the Festival, a popular mid-1980s nightspot among gay African Americans located downtown at 142 Spring Street. In 1984, the business celebrated its first anniversary with eight nights of special entertainment and parties, including performances by Lady Chablis, Tina Devore, Lena Lust, and the Family Jazz Ensemble.

African American Lesbian Gay Alliance (AALGA), 1988. Throughout the 1980s, gay African Americans in Atlanta continued to establish groups to express themselves in a city and a gay community troubled by racial tensions. At the time of its creation in the late 1980s, AALGA stood alone as the only organization in the Southeast dedicated to the concerns of African American lesbians and gays. (Photograph by Gerald Jones.)

CONGREGATION BET HAVERIM, 1988. Congregation Bet Haverim was founded in Atlanta in 1985 by a group of lesbians and gays who wanted to live openly within their Jewish faith and culture. In addition to providing a spiritual community, Congregation Bet Haverim fostered political consciousness and participation in events like Pride. (Photographer Gerald Jones.)

ATLANTA GAY MEN'S CHORUS, 1982. By the beginning of the 1980s, gay men's choruses had formed in cities across the country, including in Atlanta in 1981. Native Atlantan Jeff McIntyre served as the group's first director. In the summer of 1981, he told the *Gazette* the criteria for inclusion in the chorus were simple: a "pleasant voice" and a willingness "to use that voice to say something GOOD about being gay."

WEEKENDS ADVERTISEMENT, 1984.
Drag performer and celebrity RuPaul was born in San Diego, California, in 1960. He moved to Atlanta in 1976 and enrolled in the Northside School of the Performing Arts but dropped out within two years. Until he left for New York in 1987, RuPaul recorded songs, appeared in a local production of *The Rocky Horror Picture Show*, and starred in the 1986 Jon Witherspoon cult film, *Starbooty*.

ARMORETTES, C. 1983. The Armory attracted a large number of Atlanta Falcons fans in the late 1970s. Soon regulars formed their own informal drag troupe that put on halftime shows at the bar on Sundays. By 1980, the Armorettes were performing drag shows throughout Atlanta; around the nation in cities like New York, Miami, and Los Angeles; and in Europe.

OMNI AWARDS, 1983. The first of what would become an annual event, the Omni Awards, was held on December 8, 1983. The souvenir program explained the purpose of the event: "to foster the growth and recognition of our community's talented women." Board members included, from left to right: (first row) Deana Collins, Carol Littles, and Jean Griswold; (second row) Susan Martin, Ted Binkley, Dan Abrams, Dot Elliot, and Billy Jones. Though the board of directors selected the nominees, the public voted for the winner. The 16 award categories ran the gamut from Business Woman of the Year, Writer of the Year, and Best Dressed Woman of the Year, to Living Legend of the Year. At the first ceremony in 1983, Business Woman of the Year went to Toni Rossi, while Deana Collins received the Living Legend of the Year award. Toolulah's in Buckhead won Bar of the Year.

CRUISE, 1983. Throughout the late 1970s and 1980s, many bars and restaurants catered to a lesbian clientele. In addition to stalwarts such as the Tower Lounge at 735 Ralph McGill (formerly Forrest Road), newer establishments included Toolulah's at 3041 Piedmont Road, Arney's at 2345 Cheshire Bridge Road, and the Sportspage at 2069 Cheshire Bridge Road.

TOWER LADIES, C. 1988. One of the longest-surviving lesbian bars in the city was the Tower Lounge. It began as the Tower Drive-in Restaurant in the 1960s. In the mid-1970s, under the ownership of Betty Harris, the name changed to Tower Lounge. By that time, it had begun attracting a loyal base of lesbian customers and quickly became a center of lesbian nightlife in Atlanta.

"Atlanta's Number One Weekly Magazine– Now One Year Old"

Vol. 2, Issue 19   May 9, 1980

Thank you Atlanta for making us officially number one!

GAYBRIEL, 1979. The selection of gay publications grew in the 1970s and 1980s along with Atlanta's gay population. *Gaybriel* was a "collective, volunteer effort" to provide an "alternate style publication," according to one issue from 1979.

PULSE, 1984. The weekly publication *PULSE* premiered in 1984. In the first volume, editor Ken Austin wrote, "We believe that the publication *PULSE* is itself an historical event, and that this magazine will provide a forum from which we may continue to show one another how to be proud!" Neither *Gaybriel* nor *PULSE* survived the 1980s.

JAMES HEVERLY AND FRIENDS, C. 1983. Seen here with James Heverly (left) are Layton Gregory (center) and Fritz Rathmann. Two publications emerged in the mid- to late 1980s that became key sources of news and information for and about Atlanta's lesbian and gay community. In 1985, Patrick Coleman, Jaye Evans, and James Heverly published the first issue of *Etcetera* magazine. Within 10 years, *Etcetera* had become the largest lesbian and gay publication in the Southeast.

SOUTHERN VOICE, 1988. The year of *Etcetera*'s launch, the organization Southeastern Arts, Media, and Education (SAME) was chartered. In 1988, one of its projects evolved into *Southern Voice*. Christina Cash founded this local gay newspaper, which by the end of the 20th century was the most widely read gay and lesbian paper in the Southeast. (Photographer Gerald Jones.)

FIRST BAPTIST CHURCH, 1981. From the early 1970s to the late 1990s, Charles Stanley served as senior pastor of the First Baptist Church of Atlanta. He was also a founding member of Jerry Falwell's Moral Majority and Pat Robertson's Christian Coalition. Like many other evangelical ministers of this period, Stanley preached that HIV/AIDS was God's punishment for homosexuality, a message that could be heard on Christian radio and television stations nationwide.

JESSE BENJAMIN "J. B." STONER, 1987. Among some on the extreme right, AIDS was also commonly invoked to imply the degeneracy of racial and ethnic groups. In 1987, white supremacist J. B. Stoner led a mob that confronted civil rights marchers in Forsyth County, Georgia.

ED STANSELL, C. 1984.
A former assistant dean at Emory University, Ed Stansell (standing) was involved in several political organizations, including the Atlanta Campaign for Human Rights, a nonprofit, nonpartisan political action committee chartered in November 1984. He also actively participated in the lesbian and gay chapter of the ACLU, the Greater Atlanta Political Awareness Coalition (GAPAC), and various AIDS organizations. (Courtesy Manuscript, Archives, and Rare Book Library, Emory University.)

DAVID LOWE AND FRIENDS, 1991. In the late 1980s and early 1990s, David Lowe (pictured between Dean Greenough and Jeanne Goldie), a lawyer and graduate of Emory University, was a member of the Atlanta chapter of the AIDS Coalition to Unleash Power (ACT-UP), formed in 1988. Through condom distribution, educational efforts, and protests, the local group worked to challenge discrimination against women and men affected by HIV/AIDS. (Courtesy Manuscript, Archives, and Rare Book Library, Emory University.)

RAY KLUKA
October 23, 1952 – June 10, 1989

RAY KLUKA, FUNERAL PROGRAM, 1989. Throughout the 1980s, the city's gay publications chronicled the devastation wrought by the AIDS crisis, including the death of Ray Kluka in 1989. During the last decade of his life, Kluka was a tireless champion of gay rights in Atlanta. In 1979, he served as male co-chair of the Southeast region committee for the first national March on Washington. Over the next several years, he held leadership positions with the Atlanta Gay Center, First Tuesday Association, and Midtown Neighborhood Association and served as an editor for *Etcetera*. In 1987, Kluka received a Martha Gaines Award from the lesbian and gay chapter of the ACLU in recognition of his contributions. "Ray's gentle presence and great spirit," wrote María Helena Dolan in the July 1989 issue of *Etcetera*, "will be missed by everyone, including his family, old comrades, friends, lovers, exs and the staff here at *Etcetera*."

Four

COLLECTIVE POWER
AND CULTURE WARS
1990–2000

In the 1990s, Atlanta continued to be a magnet in the Southeast, adding newcomers to its ranks at a rapid clip. This was true for gays and lesbians as well. They moved to the city for economic opportunities, but just as importantly for its vital infrastructure of social, political, and religious organizations, businesses, and gathering places. For supporters of LGBT rights, the notion of a unified gay community was a powerful concept that could galvanize and mobilize people into action. It was a strategy equally attractive to anti-gay forces, however, which, on the grounds of "family values," sought to limit gay rights and visibility. In truth, Atlanta's community often fractured along lines of gender, race, and class. As a national gay rights movement grew stronger during the decade, LGBT Atlantans, as in other areas, discovered a new sense of collective power.

More gay and lesbian Atlantans held positions of power in their daily lives, and they did so without having to endure a closeted life. This decade saw the growth of business and professional networking groups, gay and lesbian elected officials, entrepreneurship, and local and national celebrities.

In Atlanta, lesbian, gay, bisexual, and transgender individuals proved adept at working together to challenge discrimination they experienced at home, at school, at work, and from their elected representatives. They formed strategic alliances with LGBT groups within the area and in neighboring cities and states, as well as with straight allies—families, friends, coworkers, and elected officials. And for the first time, they were operating from a position of power.

The culture wars that had risen periodically for nearly three decades flared up again in the 1990s. Pat Buchanan disparaged gays and lesbians in his speech at the Republican National Convention in 1992, as did right-wing talk radio, Georgia's U.S. representative Newt Gingrich, and the Christian Coalition, headed by Ralph Reed of Marietta. In spite of this hostile climate, gay and lesbian Atlantans increasingly chose to celebrate their unions in public ceremonies, start their own families, and pursue the happiness to which they felt fully entitled.

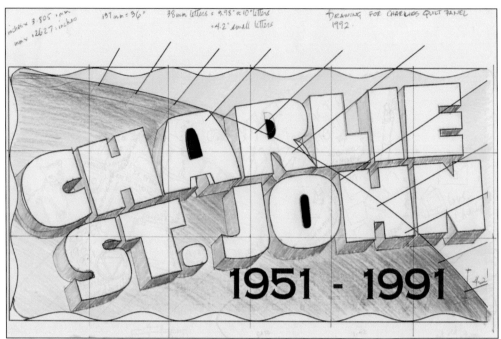

QUILT DESIGN, CHARLIE ST. JOHN, 1991. In 1972, Mayor Sam Massell appointed Charlie St. John to the Community Relations Commission, an action group with a mandate to examine and report on race relations, investigate discrimination, and recommend ways to improve human relations. St. John became the first openly gay, public appointee. A year later, he was fired from his job at the *Atlanta Journal* after handing out Gay Pride fliers.

DR. BARRY BAKER AND ALLEN JONES, 1990. Dr. Barry Baker (left), incoming president of Helping Hands, presents an award to Allen Jones, who served as president and chairman of the board of Helping Hands, an organization formed in the late 1980s to fund several AIDS service groups, including Project Open Hand and Project Outreach. In 1992, Jones created the Atlanta Executive Network, a professional networking group in service to the LGBT community.

KARL ALLQUIST, C. 1990. William Penn recognized that his partner, Karl Allquist, was not well and struggled to understand his emotional and physical withdrawal from the relationship. After developing Kaposi's sarcoma in 1990, Allquist divulged his HIV status to Penn, who discovered after Allquist's death in 1992 the journal in which he had chronicled his ordeal.

FREDDIE STYLES AND FRIENDS, C. 1993. Freddie Styles (center) embarked on his first cruise with friends George Woodard (left) and Lonnie Broughton, both of whom died in the 1990s, ending more than 20 years of friendship. For the men and women who lost family members, friends, and significant others to AIDS, such items as memorabilia, photographs, and the iconic AIDS Quilt offers both personal comfort and public acknowledgment of their loved ones' lives.

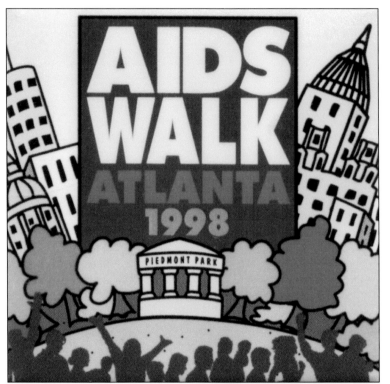

AIDS WALK PIN, 1998. In 1991, the first AIDS Walk was held in Piedmont Park with an estimated 15,000 participants. The annual event benefited AIDS organizations across the Metro Atlanta area. By the late 1990s, more than 800 corporate and community-based teams and thousands of individuals were marching. The 1997 AIDS Walk raised nearly $1.5 million for more than a dozen local AIDS organizations.

Congressman Barney Frank leads protest against Cracker Barrel, represents gays and lesbians at King Day celebrations in Atlanta

THE NEWS, MARCH 1992. After the Cracker Barrel Restaurant in Lithonia, Georgia, fired Cheryl Summerville for being a lesbian, the Atlanta chapter of Queer Nation held a protest on January 19, 1992. Hundreds attended, including openly gay U.S. representative Barney Frank of Massachusetts. Summerville's story was one of several featured in the 1996 documentary *Out at Work*, which examined antigay discrimination in the workplace.

LITHONIA, Ga. (AP)—U.S. Rep Barney Frank and 400 gay rights activists demonstrated outside a popular restaurant to protest its hiring practices.

Frank, D-Mass., joined protesters from the Queer Nation gay rights organization on Sunday, January 19, at the Cracker Barrel restaurant in Lithonia, a suburb east of Atlanta.

PAT HUSSAIN (ABOVE) AND JON-IVAN WEAVER (BELOW), 1996. In 1993, the Cobb County Commission passed an antigay resolution. In response, Pat Hussain and Jon-Ivan Weaver established Olympics Out of Cobb to pressure the Atlanta Committee for the Olympic Games to move events and sports venues from the county. Over the next few months, several protests occurred, and some even included Izzy, the Atlanta Olympic mascot. These efforts, which attracted national media coverage, led to the relocation of women's volleyball from the Cobb County Galleria Centre to the Coliseum at the University of Georgia in Athens. Hussain and Weaver chronicled their experiences in a book entitled *Olympics Out of Cobb Spiked!*, which was published in 1996.

ANTIGAY PROTESTERS (ABOVE) AND COBB CITIZENS COALITION (BELOW), 1994. After the Cobb Citizens Coalition formed in 1993, cochairs Elaine Hill and Noel Lytle called for a boycott of the Cobb Galleria Centre, which was owned and operated by the county. In her July 1995 article in *Glamour* magazine, "The Contagion of Prejudice," Patricia O'Toole described the controversy as "the beginning of a siege." "The anti-gay resolution," she wrote, "has triggered racist and anti-Semitic incidents, hurt the arts, driven away business worth millions of dollars and cost Cobb County its chance to host part of the 1996 summer Olympics." In 1997, a newly elected group of commissioners refused to reinstate the resolution.

ATLANTA PARTICIPANTS, WASHINGTON, D.C., 1993. When almost one million men and women marched for lesbian, gay, bisexual, and transsexual rights, it made national and international news. The agenda included continuing the battle against AIDS, "Don't Ask, Don't Tell," and many others. The mood of the 1987 march was angry, resulting from the failures of Reagan and Bush to adequately respond to the AIDS crisis and the Supreme Court decision in *Bowers v. Hardwick*. The third national march was noticeably more hopeful, even jubilant. For young generations of lesbian and gay Atlantans, including Andrew Parker (below, left) and Erika Linstrom (below, right), it was their first opportunity to be a part of history in the making. (Above, photograph by Alli Royce Soble.)

PARENTS AND FRIENDS OF LESBIANS AND GAYS, 1993. Shown above at the March on Washington, from left to right, are Lynne Peterson, John Meeks, Renee Palmer, and Jeri Sassany. Renee Palmer moved to Atlanta from Alabama in 1987 after being tossed out of her house because her parents suspected she was a lesbian. She attended her first Pride march in the early 1990s. There she met members of the local chapter of Parents and Friends of Lesbians and Gays (PFLAG), who changed her life—in particular, Jeri and John Sassany. They took her under their wing and became her surrogate parents. Over the years, the Sassanys' social circle came to include other "adopted" men and women, among them John Meeks and his partner, John Townsend. PFLAG Atlanta was established in the 1980s.

DIGGING DYKES OF DECATUR, C. 1994. In 1990, a group of women formed the Digging Dykes of Decatur, a garden club satirically modeled after the traditional society version. Armed with ornate floppy garden hats and plastic toy lawn mowers, they appeared in parades and protests, adding a unique brand of humor to political activism. Sherry Siclair, the "Grand Czarina," once quipped, "we're the lesbian Shriners of the parade."

STONEWALL BAR ASSOCIATION OF GEORGIA, C. 1995. The Stonewall Bar Association of Georgia, established in 1995, is comprised of lesbian, gay, bisexual, and transgender individuals and straight allies. The organization was created to bring together legal talent in the community in support of LGBT people and challenge discrimination based on gender or sexual orientation.

ATLANTA LESBIAN AND GAY HISTORY THING, 1993. Efforts to increase awareness about LGBT history in Atlanta date to the 1980s. In 1988, author and archivist Elizabeth Knowlton compiled a directory of LGBT archives. A year later, librarian and writer Cal Gough created the exhibit *Lesbian/Gay History in Atlanta*, which was displayed in the Central Library branch of the Atlanta-Fulton Public Library. Gough also put together a chronology of the city's gay past, made available to the public through the library. In the early 1990s, a group of concerned men and women formed the nonprofit Atlanta Lesbian and Gay History Thing to collect and preserve relevant sources. Today the collection forms the cornerstone of the LGBT holdings at the Kenan Research Center, the archives and library of the Atlanta History Center.

IN THE LIFE ATLANTA RECEPTION, 1996. In the Life Atlanta is the official organizer of Atlanta Black Gay Pride, which began in 1996. During the 1990s, Atlanta's African American LGBT community built relationships and organizations to bring greater visibility to the specific issues affecting black LGBT Atlantans and their families.

ADODI MUSE, C. 1996. ADODI Muse, the city's only African American gay performance poets collective, was created in 1995. Originally comprised of Duncan E. Teague (left), Tony Daniels (center), and Malik M. L. Williams, the group helped foster a safe space for the creative and artistic expressions of Atlanta's gay African Americans. Daniels died in an automobile accident in 1998, and musician and producer Anthony Antoine later joined the ensemble.

We *Celebrate the Life*
of

Ms Venus Landin

May 17, 1961 - March 2, 1993

VENUS LANDIN, FUNERAL PROGRAM, 1993. Atlanta's lesbian, gay, bisexual, and transgender community suffered an enormous loss in 1993 with the death of Venus Landin. Born in 1961, Landin, a mother of one son, filled her short years bettering the communities she held most dear, mainly through volunteer work. Landin was involved in a variety of social and political causes. She served on the board of directors for the Atlanta Lambda Community Center and as a community liaison for the 1993 Atlanta Lesbian and Gay Pride Committee. Other organizations and committees on her dossier of volunteer service were the Lesbian and Gay Task Force for the City of Atlanta, the Public Safety Committee, and ZAMI. At the time of her death at age 31, she was the co-chair of the African American Lesbian Gay Alliance.

ZAMI Pass, 1998. In 1990, a group of lesbian members of the African American Lesbian Gay Alliance voted to secede from that organization and instead create ZAMI. The name derives from a Carriacou word meaning "women who work together as lovers and friends"; it also honors the late poet Audre Lorde. In the late 1990s, ZAMI began awarding Audre Lorde Scholarships to black lesbians and gays.

ZAMI, Inc.
404 370-1392

Celebrating Black
Lesbian Scholarship

OCT 23-25, 1998
$15 WEEKEND PASS

ZAMI & HOSPITALITY ATLANTA
Invite You To An Exclusive Poetic Performance Featuring

1994 National Poetry Slam Champion...

GAYLE DANLEY
and Friends

Date & Time: Sunday September 25th, 1994, 6:00pm – 9:00pm
Place: Texas Restaurant, 10 Park Place

Following The Reading, Gayle Will Be
Signing Copies Of Her New Book NAKED

Free Admission • Refreshments Will Be Served
For More Information Call 763-9466

ZAMI and Hospitality Atlanta Invitation, 1994. Inspired by their work on the hospitality committee of the National Lesbian Conference, Charlotte Shaw, Jocelyn Lyles, and Charlene Cothran founded Hospitality Atlanta, a local African American lesbian entertainment company, in the early 1990s. Hospitality Atlanta offered recreational activities, workshops, and a supper club, and produced a newsletter.

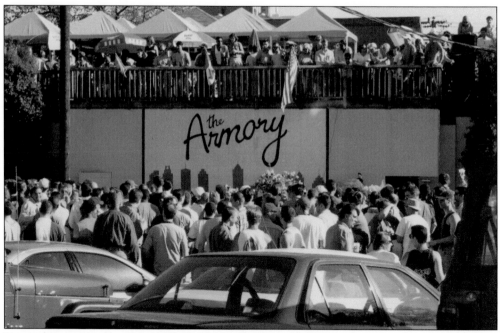

EASTER DRAG RACES, THE ARMORY, 1998. The Easter Drag Races began in the early 1980s and became a much-anticipated signature event for the Armorettes. Competitions featured participants pitted against one another to inflate condoms to the point of explosion, to toss and catch (orally) Jello shots, and to race in drag. Once held in the Armory parking lot, the tradition later moved to Burkhart's at 1492-F Piedmont Road.

OUTWRITE BOOKSTORE AND COFFEEHOUSE, 2000. In the 1990s, two bookstores served Atlanta's LGBT communities. Philip Rafshoon's dream of a community-oriented bookstore was realized in 1993 with the opening of Outwrite Bookstore and Coffeehouse. Located at the corner of Piedmont Avenue and Tenth Street, it is a mainstay of gay life in Midtown. Charis Books and More became the largest feminist bookstore in the South and continues to serve a diverse community.

MO B. DICK, MY SISTERS' ROOM, 1998. Mo B. Dick (left), the creation of New York–based actor Maureen Fischer, performed at the lesbian bar My Sisters' Room in Midtown before its move to Decatur in 1998. Although Atlanta had fewer bars catering to lesbians in the late 1990s when compared to earlier decades, those that continued to operate provided a valuable space for socializing and hosting fund-raisers and private celebrations. (Photograph by Alli Royce Soble.)

ALLI ROYCE SOBLE, 1998. Artist Alli Royce Soble (center) has been a part of the local arts scene since the late 1990s. It is a community fostered by individual artists, collectives, and theater companies whose roots go back to early pioneers like the Red Dyke Theatre. In the mid-1980s, SAME , a nonprofit arts organization, produced the literary magazine *Amethyst* and founded the film festival that became Out on Film. (Photograph by Alli Royce Soble.)

PRIDE, 1996 (ABOVE) AND 1997 (BELOW). Atlanta's Pride celebration grew during the 1990s. From 1990 to 1993, attendance rose from 5,000 to 100,000. By 1997, the number of participants in Pride had climbed to 300,000. A sign of the growth and diversity of the event, the "Welcome" in the official guide read, "Whatever your circumstances, you are about to experience one of the most powerful moments of the year in the City of Atlanta: the coming together of lesbians, gays, bisexuals, transgendered folks, and our friends and supporters, in an environment that is honoring and supportive of all." (Photographs by Alli Royce Soble.)

ORACLE CORPORATION CHRISTMAS PARTY, C. 1998. In the mid-1990s, Oracle Corporation, headquartered in Redwood Shores, California, began offering benefits to the domestic partners of its employees, including those working in the Atlanta office. In 1996, state insurance commissioner John Oxendine started a campaign against domestic partner benefits when he prohibited insurance companies based in Georgia from offering them to clients. He also attempted to prevent the Atlanta city government from granting domestic partner benefits to its employees. Eventually, the city filed suit against Oxendine. Cathy Woolard, an openly lesbian city council member, was among the plaintiffs. By 2000, however, corporations were taking the lead in providing equal benefits to their employees. That year, several Atlanta-based businesses initiated the policy, including the Atlanta Gas Light Company, the Coca-Cola Company, and Delta Airlines.

FOURTH TUESDAY MEMBERS, SPRING FLING, 1997. Fourth Tuesday, a nonprofit organization serving LBT women in Atlanta and the surrounding areas, began in the early 1980s over a business lunch. As interest grew, the group held dinners in local restaurants to accommodate the growing social and business networking circles of women. For the past 20 years, Fourth Tuesday has served the community through scholarships, educational programs, social events, and networking opportunities.

MELISSA CARTER, C. 1998. Radio personality Melissa Carter (right) began working for 99X in 1995 and contributed regularly to *Etcetera* magazine. In 2001, Carter joined "The Bert Show" on Q100, a companion station to 99X. Soon after, she became the first out morning show cohost in Atlanta radio history, charming audiences with candidness about her sexuality, as well as her battle with kidney disease.

To Cathy Woolard
With Appreciation, *Bill Clinton*

CATHY WOOLARD AND BILL CLINTON, WASHINGTON, D.C., 1999. The late 1990s witnessed several firsts for gay politicians in Atlanta. In 1997, Atlanta City Council member Cathy Woolard became the city's first openly gay elected official. In 1999, Kecia Cunningham won a seat on the Decatur City Commission as the first openly gay African American to be elected to office in the Southeast. Karla Drenner, from Avondale Estates in DeKalb County, became the first out lesbian representative in the Georgia General Assembly in 2000. The next year, the city of Atlanta elected Cathy Woolard as the city council president.

CEREMONY AT COLONY SQUARE, 1994. Seen here from left to right are Gloria Townsend, John Townsend, Charles Meeks, John Meeks, Trish Shaver, and Louise Meeks. In Atlanta, as in other cities across the country, lesbians and gays increasingly celebrated their relationships in public ceremonies in the 1990s. John Meeks and John Townsend held a large ceremony and reception at Colony Square. For Meeks, the opportunity to dance with his father at his ceremony was a cherished memory.

CEREMONY AT THE MARY GAY HOUSE, 1999. Kristal Manning (left) and Melinda McBride chose an event at the Mary Gay House, one of the few remaining antebellum homes in the Atlanta area. Their invitation began with the lyrics of Leonard Cohen's "Dance Me to the End of Love."

DELIA CHAMPION AND WENDY WEINER, KEY WEST, FLORIDA, 1999. In 1993, Delia Champion (left) and two friends opened the first Flying Biscuit Café in Candler Park with help from many friends, including Emily Saliers of the Indigo Girls. In *Biscuit Love* (2007), Saliers remembered Champion's desire for "a place where the community, in all its diversity, could gather to share meals, talk, celebrate life's milestones, read the paper, or just plain old hang out." Weiner, Champion's partner of more than 12 years, is the creative force behind the graphics that give the restaurant its distinctive look. The Flying Biscuit's popularity was immediate and long lasting. It became one of the city's top 10 restaurants and is an Atlanta landmark. In 2000, the local favorite opened its second location in Midtown and continued to garner national recognition from such publications as *Bon Appétit*, *Gourmet*, and *Zagat*, while staying true to its neighborhood roots.

BUBBA D. LICIOUS, 2000. From 1989 to 2000, Jim Marks was a member of the Armorettes and later a favorite emcee and popular host as Bubba D. Licious at special events and fund-raisers. After working with the Grady Health System, Marks served as deputy director and chief financial officer for AID Atlanta, playing a key role in helping it become the largest AIDS service organization in the Southeast. (Photograph by Alli Royce Soble.)

DIXON TAYLOR, C. 2000. In April 2000, *Atlanta* magazine honored Dixon Taylor as one of 20 "Women Making a Difference." Taylor was active in many organizations during the 1990s, including the Atlanta Executive Network, the Human Rights Campaign, and Pets Are Loving Support. Her efforts to better the lives of lesbian, gay, bisexual, and transgender individuals in the workplace included political advising and corporate consulting.

THE GENDER IDENTITY AMENDMENT, 2000. The signing of the Gender Identity Amendment marked a significant gain for transsexuals in Atlanta. Approximately 10 years earlier, the Southern Comfort Conference had begun providing support and resources for transgender Atlantans. The organization and the subject of transsexuals received significant exposure after the 2001 documentary *Southern Comfort*, which examined the life, loves, friends, and death of Georgian Robert Eads, a female-to-male transsexual.

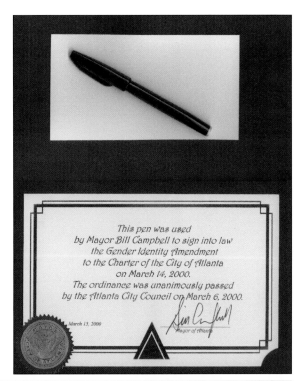

This pen was used
by Mayor Bill Campbell to sign into law
the Gender Identity Amendment
to the Charter of the City of Atlanta
on March 14, 2000.
The ordinance was unanimously passed
by the Atlanta City Council on March 6, 2000.

March 15, 2000

Mayor of Atlanta

YOUTHPRIDE, 2000. In 1995, YouthPride, the city's only LGBT organization dedicated entirely to the interests and needs of youth, was founded and supported initially by adult volunteers who sought to provide a safe and secure environment for an under-serviced age group. For the remainder of the decade, as increasing numbers of LGBT adolescents learned about the organization, YouthPride outgrew homes in both Candler Park and historic downtown Decatur. (Photograph by Alli Royce Soble.)

UNION AT MY SISTERS' ROOM, 2001. Donald Shockley (center), who served as chaplain at Emory University during the 1980s, officiated at the union between his daughter Allison Shockley (left) and Suellen Parker in April 2001 at My Sisters' Room in Decatur. Shockley's brother James and Suellen's brother Andrew, both of whom are gay, had introduced the two.

FREDDIE STYLES AND LEROY O'QUINN, 2000. Freddie Styles (left) and Leroy O'Quinn celebrated their 35th anniversary in 2000. Styles claimed that their relationship was "like a marriage. . . . We've had a normal life. In normal marriages, people go through illnesses. They go through financial problems. They get through all kinds of problems and stay together. We have done that. And we certainly deserve the rights that everyone else has. But here we are, after all these years. I can't believe it."